The Moon the Bone

Tim Metcalf

The Moon the Bone
Selected Poems 1986–2022

Acknowledgements

Thanks to my partner Jane, without whom…

Thanks to Monique Watt of Candelo, NSW,
and Professor Emeritus Kevin Brophy of Melbourne University for
assisting with the selection.

I wish to thank the many editors who have chosen to publish my poems
more than 120 times over the years. Details can be found at Trove.

A handful of poems have appeared in the UK, India, Singapore and the
USA. See my website under the Spadework link for details.

'The Good Hope' was the inaugural winner of the Rosemary Dobson Prize.

'Stages of Dying' won the 2001 W.B. Yeats (Australia and NZ) Award.

My books *Into the No Zone* and *The Solution to Us* were runners-up in
the ACT Writing and Publishing Awards (Poetry), and *Verbal Medicine*
was winner in 2006.

The Moon the Bone: Selected Poems 1986–2022
ISBN 978 1 76109 605 1
Copyright © text Tim Metcalf 2023
Cover photos by the author: front, Pilbara ironstone, heavily weathered,
WA; back, road to abandoned mine near Tennant Creek, NT

First published 2023 by
GINNINDERRA PRESS
PO Box 3461 Port Adelaide 5015
www.ginninderrapress.com.au

Contents

from Corvus
   A Brief History of Love   11
   Reaching Past   12
   Vintage cars   14
   Nocturnes, Warrnambool East   15
   Showing Bashō our bush block   17
   1,1,2,3,5,8,13,21,34,55,…   18
   A journey there and back   20
   Stages of Dying   24
   Back Ward   27
   Blue Poles   29
   Tribal   30
   The Death of Atlas   34
   Parting   35
   The trapped bird   36

from Cut to the Word
   These dead in their studied sections   39
   The most selfish person I ever met   41
   9 months Resident in Psychiatry's anti-womb   42
   Morning in the Bush   43
   can't…breathe   45
   FutureScan   46
   Fatherhood, some days   47
   The airman rolls away   48
   The Muse collapses   50

from Into the No Zone
   waking up   53
   Poet's Poet or People's?   54
   Stork's kid   55

Sadly this was not that world	56
from Molecular Pirouette	58
Our Poem	64
Not Another Flag	65
from Into the No Zone	66

from The Solution to Us

The moon the bone	69
Heading into town	70
In amongst the existential tropes	71
Love is a quantum affair	72
Self by Numbers	73
after 'What comfort for you in my name?'	74
Paranoid wind	75
A Day With Bashō	76
Profound changes in the philosophy of physics	80
'Look at him, doctor'	87
Support the head	89
Christmas 2004	90
The Good Hope	91
Ultrasound Poem #2	94
an alternative life	95
'Imagine the unthinkable'	96
Got a real job	97
Perpetual Horoscope	98
real drone	104
Two wings make the bird	105
The solution to us	106

from The Effective Butterfly

The Effective Butterfly	109
An Allemande for Horseback	110
Rodent Fugue	112

Missa Terra Nullius	114
Heat Exhaustion	115
When I'm Cleaning Windows	120
from Flying Doctor	121
Thinking about Wang Wei,	122
Letter to T'ao Chien	123
Crossing the street, avoiding a roasting	124
Making Soap	125
An Unseen Wind	127
Bega: slipping through	135
Shakespeare in Newcastle	137
Recession to a point	138
The beer lover's funeral	139

from Red Song of the Red Earth

A Rose Asunder	143
Red Song of the Red Earth	148
The Desert	152
Rare Dog Salad	154

from The Underwritten Plain

from To the reader	159
from Part I	160
from Part II	164
from Part III	168
from Part IV	172

from Numbugga Dumb Bugger

Karma Farmer	181

from Spacewalk

The Vast Importance of Knowing a Little	187
Spacewalk	189
The Racing Heart	190

Weeding Coolumbooka	191
Resurface	192
Last Stop Bombala	193

Uncollected
Black Stump	197
Mother sonnet	198
A Farewell to Country	199

from Corvus

A Brief History of Love

God or no god
there is always the future.
The Earth will turn cold,
Geology will stop.
The ocean will level the land.

The sun will flare and boil
off the seas: its implosion
will burn up the earth.
Each atom will vanish
like light from a torch
held up to the night.

The future's fixed, not worth
a thought. We've only time
to be in love. Let science
slap its head and fumble
with its facts! All the planets,
every star, will burn away.

It's taken time, it's true
to learn this answer to
the future's mystery;
but today the sun is kind,
and love still entertains
its disregard for history.

Reaching Past

Fingers

stroking skin,
sliced by knives;
probing bones
the thin ministers
of touch.

Eye

blinked, quick-fixed the image
in the inner sphere;
tossed it in the dream bowl,
the black hole:
the crucible of light.

Hand

they say
manipulated things,
waved us over here,
pulled the curtain up
on us.

Arm

reached for the cup.
Arm raised fingers to the crack,
pulled hand from the heat,
poked elbow into rib.
Arm held you too tight.

Head

was heavy, very heavy;
lolled to one shoulder.
Dead to the world, after love
the world seeped in
through holes in skull.

Brain

the perfect memory of me
and you,
and the rain,
and our wet faces.
And knowing all this.

Vintage cars

for Rebecca

I stop to watch the vintage cars go past.
I'm glad there are people who care enough
to shine them up, to lovingly preserve our heritage;
but I've never been the nostalgic type.

I'd rather race Ruby Sue (our Subaru)
up our rutted road, bang her springs
on roots and corrugations:
give her a damn good hammering

like I gave Dad's Morris back in 'sixty-three
when I was two, and he lay underneath it clanking
the diff with a spanner, and I helped on the panels
with the hammer he left gleaming in the sun.

Nocturnes, Warrnambool East

1

Old bone unburied,
tossed up on the turning earth:
full moon licked clean.

Bored hounds yawn and yap.
Mongrels sniff each other out.
Old Labradors worry azaleas.

Seagulls scrap.
Squalling cats
blow hormonal chorales.

The tide equivocates,
debates the ins and outs
of the river mouth.

Land's exhaled the day.
Night's begun
its primal argument.

2

The suburb's houses huddle
like shy debutantes, peering
through white-frocked windows.

Straining against the wind,
phone lines howl caution
to those who might surrender.

The atmosphere sways to the waves.
The looming moon is at their doors.
The world is demanding a dance.

Showing Bashō our bush block

Grey clouds stop the sun –
conversation between the
season and the day.

                              Late afternoon light
                              splays from a hole in the clouds –
                              halo over earth.

Sunset on
the hill – dusk down in
the valley.

                              No matter what age
                              who walks here – bright parrots
                              burst singing from their feet.

Still black night –
stellar infernos
churn through space.

                              Half moon tilted east,
                              galaxy arcs overhead –
                              astronomical!

Dawn valley –
cupped hands make a bowl
for the mist.

1,1,2,3,5,8,13,21,34,55,…

1

From
The
Flowers'
Petals spring
Open before us
Nature's spiralling equations
Intricate rhythms forming from simple sequences
From the single seed to the sunflower's face to the waving field
of splendid yellow
The golden centre of the picture that rapidly expanded from the
big bang through all   time until the mind of the mathematician
Fibonacci whom they called the Blockhead who found a way
that nature might have made its breathtaking rush to the Infinite
that pervades our lives that at every step confronts us and falsifies
our equanimity
That is the ever-receding-before-our-science repository of fear
and of beauty…

1

…containing the threat of innumerable possible points of departure from every event.

The other way we could consider this is to say that randomness terrifies us that our true desire is to dismantle it into predictable portions to analyse the flickering dark surrounding our fires' light

Using Quantum Mechanics to calculate our tunnelling unscathed through black uncertainties those moments into which the tiger might leap

And Chaos Theory to steady our pulse that with the forests' fractal branching trembles

Like the hands of ancients who accepted without sums

Our simple human need to grasp

This unruly world

And reduce

It all

To

One.

A journey there and back

Tyres and tarmac having parted we were up,
prop thrust west to sundown
beyond which the woman lay
skull-thumped flat to Ramingining dirt.

Everything else fell away:
airstrip, hangars, Gove town and its hospital
where I'd tried to see her
through the silences between words
that spoke the apprehension of a nurse
also seated by a radio.

So now I was flying,
heartbeats and adrenalin enough for two.
I thought of us as nosing out
into the slipping stream of atmosphere,
crossing rivers and escarpments,
chasing the sun to get there in time.

Reality was less romantic.
The Nomad was losing its struggle
against gravity and spin.
The Earth dragged us backwards from the day.
The rivers silvered then vanished
through night's void reflection.

Had I stepped outside
I would have seen a cabin of plastic and tin
vibrating across the sky;
a pilot suspended like a mind's eye
in space before his luminous dials;
lit windows and silhouettes;
a nurse reading her magazine;
a young doctor studying a book,
fumbling with a trepanning drill,
thinking to himself that out here
the only reference point is me;
and this plane beginning to fall.

Flickering yellow lights appeared:
five gallon drums of kero defining a runway.
A crescendo of noise. Rubber scuffing dust.
A crescendo of silence. A corridor of flame.
A nurse walking through firelight, beckoning.
Sound of voices reappearing. A reversing vehicle.
Cacophonous battle: Land Rover versus potholes.
Rattling teeth and bones.
Fragmented sentences…no power…fruit
bats in the generator shed…
not alcohol, not kava…
Eye whites by torchlight.
Night black as night, blacker.
A body breathing, sometimes.
Glinting instruments.
Scraping feet.

Some words.
Some minutes
Passing.

Then briefly the lights on. Off.
The doctor standing, saying
'leave now or stay to die'.
The woman unasked on the stretcher.
The Land Rover crashing back.
Engines and burning flares
raising an island from the darkness.
Doors sealed, cabin lights full power.
Silence muted. The plane lifting off again
into night's fast-flowing river.

Back inside we plugged in: oxygen,
intravenous mannitol to shrink her swollen brain,
a catheter to drain the fluid off.
Vital signs stable, then unstable then…
somehow the woman like a body half-submerged
bobbing to the surface, up, down again,
coming closer; a form more distinct,
a pattern to the wavering of pulse and respiration…
For hours we anticipated
the flicker of an eyelid.

I remember when she opened her eyes
because dawn, which had overtaken us unseen,
now strode before us, and lit up Darwin:
all bright orange glass reflecting.
I put the unused drill back in its bag
and closed the book.
She murmured, and I thought
that success is measured more
by what you don't have to do.

Stages of Dying

(after Elizabeth Kubler-Ross)

denial

In anatomy class
we cut textbook lines
into the dull clay of our body.
We shook dismembered hands,
and bragged of cricket with arms and balls
for a joke.
We washed the formalin from our hands
for the next two days.

shock

A pregnant girl collapsed.
The scalpel cut quick and deep.
Her grey belly peeled apart.
The monitors ticked:
a mechanical requiem.
White gloves pulled out the baby
cold and dead like the streets
I wandered half that night.

guilt

As an intern
I was anxious, and obedient.
To cure at all costs
was the boss' creed.
I had no time for the old woman
we made betray her faith.
Soon after the transfusion
she died of cancer.

anger

Some drunken bastard
hit this woman with his car.
Her young breasts quivered
each time we thumped her chest.
Over half an hour
her face, burned alive,
set cold, branding for life
the mind of her child.

sorrow

Was it happy, his final memory?
This poor bloke, purple-faced
and next in line for death?
I was naive, yesterday,
regarding his broken heart.
Today it wouldn't go any more.
Tonight I was drunk.
There were tears, briefly.

acceptance

I went to see an elder on his beach up north.
He didn't say much.
There was this sky-blue dreaming;
the ocean its lucent mirror,
flawless like an egg.
I heard he died around sunset.
That night a warm breeze blew
the soothing tune of the sea.

Back Ward

Next, an old man spilling pills:
a burnt-out schizophrenic;
a dribble-bibbed dyskinetic
watching TV, one slow pupil
30 still frames behind.

They say one day he just rode off
on one of his inventions,
a badly drawn contraption,
turning back briefly to scoff
at his body deserted by mind.

The truth is he's still inside,
a man so timid and drugged
that you can strut right up and tug
at his flesh: he has no pride,
no anger, no life to find.

To meet this man is to fall
down his stare without resistance
into an empty pit. There's no insistence
on respect, no ego at all.
You feel as if you're blind

to his suffering, but that's not right:
there's no person that reacts.
I fear the chasm's edge, reject
it angrily. I will not fight
for life for him, nor pass his time.

I can do nothing more.
There is no one to grab onto,
to bravely haul back up into
the world. All I can do is ensure
the orders are dated and signed.

Blue Poles

Slashed by glass,
by the angry hand;
rent to empty space
the lacerated canvas flaps.

A blue-poled trail
        staggers
through the neon blizzard
of an alcoholic mind.

Deepest blue
ice-cold fissures cut
        deceptive steps;
tangle-spanned chasms.

Navigate the hazed cloud
of brain by its scars,
its torn electric-blanket vision
of reality no longer warm.

Tribal

after Sir James Fraser, *The Golden Bough*, concerning South America

       Plump fruit elliptical pendulums.
Fat flick-footed monkeys leap
branch to bough down now away
through history's dank horizons.
Stems sway, swivel, fray, unravel
backwards in time, forwards in evolution.
Husks plummet, split, spill
 their seeds that slither like memories
from the shaman's skull, club cleft
in the season of the sacrificial.

       One time he saw a spirit.
It was leaving a woman's body,
a stream of shrieking pouring out
into a vessel: floor of earth,
wall of chanting women,
vortex for the waters and the blood;
and the baby the colour of the moon,
of the soul looking back
before flying home to the stars.
He saw terror clutch the throats
of the women, fly screaming
with them through the trees.
He saw the mother tear her flesh free
and scrabble up the torrent of her blood
to death.

      Then the spirit cried out
from its new mouth, and the young man
hiding in the jungle heard its voice.
He threw his club aside, put the girl
to the ripe fallen breasts.
She drank. He ran his fingers through her skin;
he wondered if her blood was milk.
She slept, and the spirit was quiet.

      He thought of his master, withered,
hung with poisons and pieces of death,
and of his master's death cradled now
in his arms; and of the way
his testicles would taste,
and the mother's cold tongue.

      As the seasons heaped around him,
he sat and watched her.
Her sacred footsteps stirred no dust
in the village; in the jungle
she ate freely of the fruit
as snakes slithered silently away.
She thanked no spirit and was not punished.
She was happy and would dance before him
squatting morose at his door,
lost in the time that must come.

      In that season many spirits rose up,
their giving fists clenched tight
in angry accusation.
They demanded her return.
She threw back her head and laughed:
he trembled inside his mask.

      Mock solemn, stepping lightly as a cloud
she walked the corridor of stamping feet,
poking hipbones, rattling teeth.
Wide-grinned faces tossed her up
into the sky, she cried out
in delight and whirled and whirled
about then hurled onto the heap
of golden corn stretched out
basking in her glory dancers
dancing in and out and
pulsing in and out and
around and around
the leering world swirled
and delirious with life
she drank the warm blood flowing
from her slit throat,
and saw her final sight
fading from her eyes:
the masked shaman's penis swaying.

   He saw her spirit to the stars
then returned, to find the whole world
shrunk to a hilarious circle,
teeth screeching in his face.
He was alone.

   He carried her head always.
The gaping mouth was dry.
It seemed to thirst for his soul.
He gave freely, and in return
living memories followed him
into each night. Her feet stamped
across his chest, her laughter caught
the winds in his throat.
His spirit withered until he knew
his time had passed.

   Outside idly swinging his club
the next shaman stood waiting
for the final story.
Inside the old man gazed once more
at his girl then called him in,
ordered that his heart be his first feast,
then, with a long look of lost peace
set forth the last great story,
the one he braved all worlds to tell,
to alter forever,
so that the girl could live.

The Death of Atlas

An odd name for a small dog,
but you did your best
to stop the turning world.

Spittle-foamed lips drawn back,
muzzle thrust in the dirt,
snarling at the cruellest leash

your tortured eyes
turned back to chase
the final wombat down its hole.

Everything was too big for you
but you barked anyway,
in the growling cavern of the end.

Little digger,
you made it hard for death
all along the gutter's rough.

Parting

In the silent sky green forest
in the valley of a leaf
a mist of anguished minutes
trembles in the veins.

Condensing to a final hour
a drop of crystal moment hangs,
then stretching turbid with the weight
of yearning falls away

down through dark tormented space
to splat in inky black upon
the dead dry bony whiteness of
a too soon turning page.

The trapped bird

Carefully,
lest I crush

the tiny sticks
of bone

I extend
my enormous hand.

For one beat
fingers touch.

Wings thrust out
to freedom

so light

weighing
almost nothing.

from **Cut to the Word**

These dead in their studied sections

We were introduced, gently,
to the volunteer dead
who turned their bodies over to the scalpel-blades
of science and education.
Their leisurely dissection afforded ample time
to feel the cold silken fat beneath skin;
the pickled flesh textured like old steak.
We sketched potted body bits,
horror-drawn to the woman
slivered head to toe in one-inch slabs.
I reckoned she was close
to bearing her grey baby.

These dead in their studied sections
left their impressions in our young minds
but never so incisively as those
who struggled in our newly graduated hands
with their trauma: the violent head-shot,
the car-smashed and knife-struck;
the steel-gouged, truck-ruptured and train-cut;
from farms the cow-crushed, horn-gored,
back-snapped and power-take-off-shafted;
the grey burnt-alive in their ghastly cloud;
the blood-blistered sand-suffocated;
and the drowned, reef cut and swilled in body bags.

Most who die don't struggle.
Death has humbler ways:
failed and fevered organs, numb comas,
cancer's flesh-plug pulled and lives drained away;
the prompt departure of hearts long-caged
in hard-artery nets drawn suddenly tight;
the master-strokes that kill the brains.

The professional endures, with their patient
frustrated incapacity
the flop of limbs and organs;
waits until some industrious micro-organism
claims the body for its temporary citadel
and coughs its tiny satellites of death
into a hospital ward thick already
with its spores.

Death, seen so often, takes nothing from us,
miraculously kills none
of our own death's desire:
to find our body in its bed, at home
one early bird-filled morning,
woken up, as they say,
dead.

The most selfish person I ever met

'Hey! I was here before her!'
Right in my face the fat lady snarls.
She's been stabbed in the belly.
Pointing angrily to the bloody slit
she loudly tells her waiting time.
I glance at the ECG. It is steady.
Miranda leads her back to bed.
Everyone calms down again.

It's natural to feel afraid, upset,
angry that you have been stabbed
then left on a casualty bed
with the lights turned down.
The knife might have killed
a thinner person.

Standing up and yelling in my face
is sound clinical evidence
of reasonable immediate health.
Frowning slightly I nod to Johnson.
Once more the woman between us
jolts. The ECG stays dead steady.

9 months Resident in Psychiatry's anti-womb

I held my breath
and dived in, headfirst

but remained submerged
in the miserable ocean

the surface lost and no one
to throw me a rope.

I sank, fearing my skull's
implosion

white water thoughts
in the black depths

a turbid time
to decide

to break and settle
in the heavy mud

or to rise one mind,
clear as water.

Morning in the Bush

The currawongs advance
branch by branch.
Black wings slit the canopy
(sky blue, leaf green).
Glinting eyes try
to outstare the man
walking amongst their trees.

Black scythes slash the day.
Down pours that night:
wind-lashed trees drop flowers
like sobs for the life
you snatched away.

Koori woman,
stolen child,
where is my innocence?
Did you know I couldn't see
the suicide in your smile?

I hated death
as the young doctor should.
I thought I held you up.
I fell so hard.
Where were the tablets I gave you?
The books I read?

You cut me with your truth.
My grief was not for you.
Now the wind
is only cold, and I know
I don't belong, here,
amongst the trees
or the birds
that keep their careful distance.

can't…breathe

In tense moments
I wish my stethoscope
was all they want it to be:
two steely serpents
unwound from the physician's staff,
whispering answers
in my ears.

Reflected in the sterile metal
I see this differently:
forehead tethered to a frown
by ostentatious earrings
weighing me down
like question marks
in lead.

FutureScan

The ultrasonic probe
gathers echoes
scattered from the womb.

The child to survive the mother,
a grey blur in a pixel pool,
swims up to the screen.

'Look! It's waving at me!'
We count ten fingers wriggling
like metaphors.

'Can you see what sex it is?
Can you see what colour sheets
Mum should buy?'

The foetus curls up,
hands over its ears:
the world's too loud yet.

Beam off, the room is dark.
In the cathode glow we watch baby
kick the glistening belly.

Fatherhood, some days

I come home from work
and there it is: the family;
the oldest crying

at the youngest crying
at her mother's anger
at her crying

and the bare brick walls,
and the bored yap
of the mutt next door.

Everything seems naked.
I stand guilty
in my working clothes

thinking angrily
of the day
I have already faced.

The airman rolls away

I have always found conversation a little stifled when wiping clean the papery skin of the incontinent. First my potential partner in conversation is rolled away with their back to me; and second trying to hold my breath disrupts the natural flow of words and the pauses in between them. So I say little, mouth breathe to avoid the smell, and ask myself the same question over and over again: 'where is the poem in this?'

I take the weight of the upper buttock. My thoughts turn to the action heroes in those films. How come they never stop to go? First there is no time; and second it isn't in the script. In reality we know the toilet break is often simultaneous with the climax, at which point the hero's bowels let go, as in the Spitfire cockpits of World War Two. Funny they never mention the Messerschmitts.

It's adrenalin that keeps the hero flying, and us sitting comfortably through the film; any turd we may have formed perched unobtrusively on a ledge in the colon. It's evolution that keeps it up there without us knowing. Adrenalin shuts down everything excess to alertness, works the heart harder, pumps itself around the body. It readies the big muscles, opens the pupils wide in the weird theatre light.

It's evolution that expels the turd at the crisis, the point of death assumed. I wonder why that is, too. Evolutionary efficiency? Our minds set against our excrement, the stench of our own kind. No nutritional value in our shit.

My work reveals the lax anus, the colour of toothless gums, a pouting mouth hung open between words. I wonder if it's owner's brain was up his arse before he was laid flat. As his mates might have joked. Somewhere up this shit-smeared orifice, wandering the slick intestinal passages.

The inner man flies direct to the cranium. It is wordless now. All expression poured into the bed.

Shit is evidence of life when the brain is wordless. If it keeps coming we have beaten our old adversary. Adrenalin kept this old airman alive through the long war. Intravenous adrenalin kept him alive through this stroke that took out half his brain in one hit. A final swipe between his emaciated buttocks, then he's dried off, and rolled back onto clean sheets, and fluffed pillows his soft clouds. 'There we are,' I say, unconvincingly nonchalant.

He understands but doesn't speak. Perhaps that's true of everybody some of the time. I would not project my thoughts into his world, no matter how blank it seems. I act busy, professional. I gag silently behind his back to preserve some dignity for both of us. Not that I will recall his name; only his dying skin like a paper screen for a movie flickering in a hospital room.

The Muse collapses

Lifting my lady's delicate hand
gazing into her bewildered eyes
I murmur 'I'm sorry.
I know this will hurt'
then slap her veins hard at the wrist.
I watch her wincing,
weakening.

Her pulse is difficult to find.
Her heart's
alive
its rhythm
erratic.
Lying in a pool of blood
she needs some fluid yesterday.
I rip packets open,
ready an intravenous drip
but there's no one about to help.

'Damn and curses,
where are the nurses?'
I expostulate, to make conversation.
She looks at me blankly.

The woman has no poetry
in her blood.
I slap her again,
slip in a line,
squeeze the bag hard.

from **Into the No Zone**

waking up

Yes yes,
the dawn:
it is beautiful.
I try to miss it.

Each morning
is different.
The poet
cannot compete.

Cocooned
in the wonderful
world
this morning

it is too early
to choose
which bird,
which cloud.

Wet skins pressed
together in our bed,
what is it worth
to open my eyes?

Poet's Poet or People's?

I can't say.

To elaborate, I think creating a Spurious Dichotomy will Inevitably lead my brain towards the slow-wheeling Vortex of Meaning.

There are two and only Two Possibilities, if and only if Zen.

That, and then This, is how I see it.

The first (or second) is nothing, and one (or The Other) is that Everything; is that Absolute is not. Everything that is true is in its own right. No perspective may be neglected.

The Not-Vortex turns out, to be the Night Template of the Vortex.

Poetry and Poetics! That Sensation of Vertigo. Ride it through to the Central Stillness, the Source of Desire, our Need to Speak. This could be an argument for something, and or nothing. No point, no infinity, no silence. Never mind.

I argue/s for something. For taking action. For primary Production of the Poem. For its Primal Primacy. For its Existence is Spite of Not. To emit my Crashing Sound like the Quantum Forest that both fell and did not fall.

This for the sake of argument, nothing more.

Stork's kid

Never mind who my parents were.
They dropped me off down here
on their way to somewhere else.

Barren, fascinating land,
no wonder they were torn
Between it and all the other places.

I dried out quickly
after birth in the sun;
skin with a feeling for stone,

ears attuned to the magpie's song,
black and white, and all the other birds;
the raven's caw of emptiness.

I tried homecoming, flying
to their home. There were too many people,
and the seasons too obvious.

I came back, like a boomerang,
to the corrugated iron and dust,
the animals dead on the side of the road,

their bewildered companions
standing around for a while
and wandering away,

more aimless orphans
looking for food in the echoing rooms
in the great silent house of Australia.

Sadly this was not that world

Today the second goldfish died.
There was no grief to speak of.

I thought there should be a poem about this:
two goldfish, taken from their indoor bowl of years
to an outside pond, then dead within days.

I thought there should be meaning to this;
a metaphor perhaps
for expanding our horizons too far,
like the time outback
I lay down and stared up at the stars
until I felt myself reduced
to a point in space
as tiny and as far away as they are,
and, like them, hurtling away from the others.

Then I sensed the infinity that is the universe
and shrank back inside my self
with a frightened snap.
Suddenly my skin was too cold
for feeling. Though I knew this
as mere sensation,
I crawled into my sleeping bag
and shivered on the verge of being
all that night.

In the morning there was ice over everything.
Bare mountain rock was breaking up
the desert sky's flawless rim.
Warped sediments, orange and red in the dawn sun,
cut a compass for my mind
a sand and stone affirmation
of self in body centred,
on the flat expanse, walking
on the flagstone floor of the atmosphere:
not floating, lost, like the fish.

Exactly why they died
I'm uncertain. They had a large rock,
and a hollow log.
Maybe their lighter minds
are easily sucked out into space
to recede forever with the stars
in every possible quantum world,
except the one in which I find a way to warn them,
so that when next submerged in moonless night
they need not drown in emptiness,
in the absolute cold of space.

Sadly this was not that world,
and of the three of us
only I survive, to believe I defy
gravity, hilarious belief, and the infinite.

from Molecular Pirouette

7 DNA: Did Not Attend. The science of divorce

DNA made me leave my wife
after hers had zipped up mine
and we had created two healthy offspring;
vigorous hybrids of their parent stock.

The behaviour of this molecule!
The power of genes to make us fat,
stupid, alcoholic, or psychologically fit
for life in a dysfunctional family:

whatever we choose to believe.
My DNA did what it evolved to do
then left me here in its body,
its self-perpetuating metabolic factory

running way beyond breaking even,
long enough to watch our children sprint
up the hill behind the shed, where last year
I found some crimson felt beneath some leaves.

Several scientific departments later
we discovered no taxonomist alive
could identify my 'felt' past *Eriophyses*:
a genus of the blister mite.

Furthermore, the leaf it lived on
was probably not what I thought it was,
twenty percent of plants in the bush
being hybrids: species I found

are obsolete, a Renaissance persistence
of strict categorisation adapted
to our information age
hungry for packaged knowledge.

Hybrids spread the risk:
genetic variation
the robust lubricant for life
on this cog-stone Earth

in this universe turning and returning.
My daughters run back down the hill
innocent of my meditations.
They ask me questions

I tell them there is nothing really complicated
about our story; or amazing, or different;
only it's in the curious language of science; the details
of me breaking up, and her getting even.

8 X-ray crystallography

For Emily

Trying to see what's on
without a crick in the neck
bending over primitive equipment
Franklin and others crystallised DNA.
Bouncing x-ray beams off their biological gems
they projected patterns onto screens.
Mathematical analysis was the next layer
of their painstaking portrait
of deoxyribonucleic acid.

X-ray Crystallography is far too hard.
Today Scanning Tunnelling Electron Microscopes
map the surfaces of molecules.
Automatic sequencers and computer algorithms
construct the picture so much faster.

I feel her attention drifting.
Bring it back to the perceptible world.

DNA is a double helix,
like spiral pasta before they cut it up
into bite-size pieces.
Some of the smallest living things, under the microscope,
are spiral bacteria. There are tiny worms
and seed cases, and cocoons in the soil
if you look, and some are always spiral shaped,
just like water down a drain or vines up a tree.

Her feet shift. My daughter has had enough of this.
Perhaps I expect too much of a four-year-old.
Finish quickly.

There's a sort of basic maths to the universe,
and a bio-maths to DNA
and they are all based on the sine wave
which is very simple
but which can get incredibly complicated
like a tree, or a horse
or a person.
It's everywhere,
as the patterns of nature.

She is shuffling her feet about now.
Looking up I meet her crystal-clear eyes
her cheeky face grinning
framed by curls she has crammed
beneath a cardboard-box hat.

12 Nestlings of indeterminate appearance

Woe betide the tadpoles, *Lymnodynastes fletcheri*,
netted by my girls for investigation
into the mystery of growth,

the disgust at decay:
for few will live to spawn.
400,000 eggs in their ovaries

swell with the girls to twirl
in skirts, and try their mother's
brown-eyed looks at boys

(that may not go well
as both have my iris:
grey-blue and serious).

Spin they will, in the dance,
like the molecules of life
in the metabolic maelstrom,

generative turbine whirling
further in and further out
centrifugal within our solar space

and somehow, dizzily spinning too
all around my daughters is love,
all that is known and that is passed on.

So what do I say to them?
We did our best within biology's
contemporary constraints?

I'm sorry people's lives
sometimes spin apart?
Be creative with your DNA?

Our Poem

You ring me up to tell me
the girls don't want to come around this weekend
because I never do their hair properly
and they to have make their lunch for school.

I promised myself to speak in love only.
There is hate to resist. I have been breaking
my word from the day I was born. You push me
for that poem I have not written yet.

Not Another Flag

A
knob
on
a
p
o
l
e

then the flag flapping / about the legs
in the wind / the legs / in khaki trousers
caked with blood and flies / the dead men
oh how they died / brave heroes / to a man
the women fell apart/ the children exposed
the cruel world stepping through/ wall TV
selling the myth / the flag again
with the valiant ensign / leading the attack
over the top to plant the flag / for all

t
o
s
e
e
t
h
e
p
l
a
c
e
t
h
e
y
d
i
e
d.

from **Into the No Zone**

Warp One. Disengage.

Into the No Zone
where you control the action
enter any character

point and click to register
the disapproval of suits
going up

windows everywhere
stacked executive support
officers filter all water

hide acquisition errors
in real-time dialog boxes
stand silent in elevators

ascend, cope, descend,
exit, breathe out.
Implacable visor

take out the pavement
look cool in the queue
& weather the news.

from The Solution to Us

The moon the bone

The moon the bone most picked over,
clean as space, white as a grin;
no silver spills, the moon's no lover,
or mover (it is Earth that spins).

Though like the trees we're rooted dumb,
the moon now lifts, now lays us down
unshaken, trusting day to come,
and gravity to hold its ground.

Drought-killed branches in the lunar wind
are time's dark hands waving from the clock…
I turn away from them and come back in,
close the door on space and night and rock,

on my thoughts too like them, and load this wood
to warm you up, my love, my living moon.
Autumn firelight makes you look so good
in your woollen jumper in our room.

Heading into town

High energy physicists, colliding particles,
might generate a black hole to consume us
in less than the seconds remaining
to my bursting from the tunnelling bush
into mid-winter pasture,
sunlight skating off frost
then Bang! diffracted
by the dust-pitted windscreen
so that, at this time of year,
there is always a passage of faith
where I hold the wheels straight,
squint for animals and then
accelerate into the blindness.

In amongst the existential tropes

In amongst the existential tropes
between eccentric and insane,
humble simultaneous with vain,
my body alternately grins and mopes.
It struggles against the random world,
fears that chaos might take the reins
and steer off course, for all my pains,
the wrong flag flapping, that I unfurled.
I tolerate the hills and dales
to achieve one day the open plains,
soft repose in horizontal lanes;
to circulate when life inhales;
to rest and breathe at ease, one hopes,
in amongst the existential tropes.

Love is a quantum affair

strange attractor
i didn't understand, myself
as a charm quark
probably spinning a dream
awake the energy welling up
i wanted to, in principle
i was uncertain
once you made the observation my lips are soft
(though i don't always shave)
one kiss and the world shifts
but at the same time (different place)
and/or the same place (different time)
or neither
it doesn't antimatter.

Self by Numbers

Subtracting the actual murderers,
the potential killers and their sycophants,
those beaten to silence as a child,
and the everyday suffering folk;

subtracting the cynical, the disillusioned,
the insanely happy, the socially brilliant,
the determined philanthropists
and the innately hopeful throng;

subtracting to a flickering somebody
trying to glimpse another
who by waving 'Hello!' back
can confirm the observation

that no one by themselves
can prove a single thing.

after 'What comfort for you in my name?'

by Alexander Pushkin

In my heart lives all the world.
I let it in, it was in need.

I cannot mention all the names,
ripples on a globe of blood.

When I sing I channel voices
from every place and every time.

They have died all our deaths.
It comforts me to know the tune.

I cannot sing for very long,
I don't remember all the verses.

History awaits me too.
The poem will carry us secure.

Paranoid wind

Six weeks of you, wind.
You are drying out the world.

The stars have burnt and fallen
to the cracked mud floors of dams.

Logs block tracks, and daylight
sharpens shadows over stones.

Hungry for paranoid feed
I know it's you, wind, slamming doors

swivelling leaves from silver eyes
to green sardonic smiles.

I won't jump or rattle.
Ruffle parrots. Hassle trees.

The animals concur:
we'll wait you out, and anyway

we are all being watched:
the spider by the wasp

the lizard by the butcherbird,
the eagle by the satellite

the man in the uniform
by his overseer, her overseer

the watchers of the watchers,
the whisperers, and you, wind

wind that sometimes howls
from the hidden mouths of trees.

A Day With Bashō

Morning mist:
land lulled by water's
softest voice.

Winter is dismal here.
Dead wet logs are slippery and black.
Tiger leeches bunch and release,
bunch and release.

The best light falls inside warm rain,
Long, and late in spring. Autumn is fine too.
Such clarity.
The mist will rise.

Full spectrum fanfare!
Dawn's prism, sun's bell clanging,
songbirds singing day.

That's a magpie.
We get a number of species here:
Sulphur-crested cockatoos,
Gang-gangs, raucous galahs.

There are superb blue wrens,
parrots and rosellas, corellas,
treecreepers, honeyeaters, kookaburras, ducks;
but we're out of luck: it's winter.

Lonely white farmhouse.
Clouds and sheep and cockatoos
flocking over fields.

Not any more mate!
The paddocks are trussed up.
The world's curled into itself,
 yet lonely as the satellites

we launched to watch over it.
We have built a lot of fences.
We want to know the details.
Make a record of each event.

Sky of rain.
Blue tractor idle
in the shed

Flash of blue:
parrot, tractor, a patch of sky?
I see the colour running,
as in veins, back to the heart.

Listen to me! One word from you
And I can't stop talking!
You can't connect
the lines like that!

Cold basalt outcrop:
once fired in the volcano,
ever defiant.

Forever doesn't exist these days.
It's all probability.
Field potential.
Quantum fluctuation.

Scientists have resolved the empty spaces.
Dark energy pervades them all.
Stasis is a defunct illusion.
There's no such thing as nothing.

Winter night.
One trillion stars:
I stand here freezing.

One Earth over zero space
equals infinity.
It's a mathematical trinity:
self-centrifugal fascination.

Mandala times Mandelbrot
equals introspection.
We spiral in away
from your Zenith-less Zen.

Yellow square on black:
farmhouse facing moonlit clouds
billowing at night.

It's cold. It's move or shiver.
It's the animal in me.
Stacking words like this to build a fence.
Let's talk over it like neighbours.

Everything evolves
a falsehood born of itself.
Progress is by paradox.
You too wrote down your poem.

*Drive on! The white-faced
heron, mirrored there, feeds on
self-reflection.*

Profound changes in the philosophy of physics

'But what can be contrary to the mind
which holds all contraries in concord still?'
Sir John Davies: *Nosce Teipsum*

1

Sun's up, as predicted
and the observable world
sets to setting right
the chaos of the night.

2

Birds reweave the fibres sprung
from their nests, feed their chicks.
Someone says the morning's still,
walking in the apple orchard,
the humdrum drone of wasps and bees
like busy humans stocking larders,
the coming clatter of the parrots,
and I am feeling like an apple
trying to hold the tree together.

3

As apple and not-apple,
simultaneously,
there is no stem to grapple,
I'm falling, suddenly…

4

…it's apple roulette with energy wells,
buckets shuffling back and forth
to catch and hold me, *terra firma*,
my anxious self staring down,
the chosen bucket winding up,
my face reflected in its water.
The apple hits! The ratchet cracks
and plummets the apple, the bucket and me
through rippling complexity
to dark to black
to nix

5

still
falling

6

the bucket's now behind me,
the well-shaft opens like a bell
and flips! And peels away
like lifting off from Einstein's nose,
and here's another universe,
black at first, but I see stars,
dull red giants I seem to know,
planetary apples, each in orbit
round the other, each a face
at once its own and every person's,
here now's Isaac Newton, he and I,
parallel and intersectable,
pondering ecliptic decay,
the force on falling bodies,
the impact at coordinates
of his apocryphal cranium;
and why not the ground beside him?
Absent-minded, he strokes the apple,
which when he isn't looking purrs:
it's Schrodinger's cat,
so that it was never purely apple
and the stalk…

7

Abruptly there are people in the orchard,
talking about burning the dead timber
how Giordano Bruno crackled in the fire.
Their voices agitate and heat the air,
the apples hover, rise to join their trees,
but under every leafy shadow lurks
another quirky universe and then
the orchard and the people and the fruit
recede so fast from me
my cries can't catch them.

8

floating mind, quantum questions,
to which, circling the apple-sphere
I cling:
'Why, and why not?
When, where and what?
Which, no need to choose.
How indeed! You lose!'

9

A bite-size cosmos
Flies alongside.
Here kinetic energy
of the falling apples
cooks the pies!
I'm frightened now.
All I hear is a rope
unravelling
into the yes/no void
of the roiling mind.

10

Infinite Space

11

Yes/no. No! No thing.
Keep talking!
Yes/no. Don't let go!
Keep talking!
It's getting too hot, we're going to boil!
Keep talking! Chaos will dissolve us!

12

I'm back in the bucket, bobbing,
an apple trying to bite itself,
a furious, endless drowning,
fighting the entropy, feeding it,
I lunge for a straining hand,
it's Sergeant-Major Poetry
screaming fierce commands:
I'm ordered back to the bell,
up the shaft, out of the well,
and I'm flat out,
gasping,
the orchard's a parade ground,
the apple trees espaliered,
his face is red, he's at my ear:
'Knock it around.
Slap it about.
Regiment it,
Round it out.
Yes. No. Yes. No…'

13

he marches me off
bawling 'Fall out!
It's time to wind down.'
Trembling I ask for
a lift into town.
He hasn't a car.
Says hitching's best.
It seems fear's a freeway
right through my chest.
I find I have fingers
and find I'm in luck,
a woman with apples,
a delivery truck,
she's coming from market
to replenish the trees,
she hands me a boxful
to hang as I please…

14

I'm through and sit silent,
a bird chips and flits,
in my eyes the sun rises,
I reach for the dark glasses,
a falling apple glistens.

'Look at him, doctor'

'Look at him doctor, his nose runs green,
it's all I can do to keep his lip clean.
He's a fever as well, and is off his drink,
there's something not right, I'm approaching the brink!

We've always had dinner promptly at five.
If he misses a meal do you think he'll survive?
I watch his breath, he can't breathe all night,
I'm worried to death and dying of fright.'

The child she describes looks grumpy but well,
in a minute or so he'll start to raise hell.
Look at his ears and his nose and his throat;
recite the remedies, teaching by rote.

The doctor who cares will look twice at this mother,
she's told you one problem, but there is another.
Why's she so anxious about a mere cold,
here so often with her four-month-old?

Beware of dismissing this trivial case,
look hard in her eyes, the lines on her face,
she's young: the answer's not buried too deep.
Ask her gently; you may see her weep.

Between husband and baby she gets no rest.
They both want her time, they both want her breast.
Her mother-in-law hassles day-long,
and all that she does is utterly wrong.

Look at her doctor, her eyes are red.
The treatment's to listen to each word that's said.
To take care of the baby, take care of its mother.
See her outside…then show in another.

Support the head

When we heard what was coming
my pregnant nurse paled.
Out of character, she agreed
to being sent away.
We called another nurse instead.
Support the head.

Poor father: backed his four-wheel drive
across his toddler's chest and skull;
a silent wife, unconscious child.
Though its lips were blue and dull
the needle let the blood still red.
Support the head.

We somehow calmed the parents:
'At that age they're flexible.'
They watched us work and sweat and worry.
'He'll soon be out of hospital.
No guarantees, it must be said.'
Support the head.

At last the helicopter came.
The kid did well, his parents coped.
Casualty happy, a good day's work.
Some of us drank, or cried, or smoked,
but few could rest in mind or bed.
Support the head.

I could not rest in mind or bed.
I could not monitor myself.
Nobody monitored me.
I never had my mental health.
Support the head.
Support the head.

Christmas 2004

When the tidal wave heaved over, did you feel the frightened souls?
I was struggling with my shopping bags at Coles.

What about Iraqis breathing wartime's bloody fog?
I was cutting steak to feed my dog.

Why imprison Afghans, who fled a stern God's face?
Refugees won't help me find a parking space.

Do you think poetry should always come from pain?
I read it once. Never again.

What about all mankind's folly, poets not exempt?
I don't care. Another beer?
                    Good idea, my friend!

The Good Hope

i

At the Good Hope Hospital, in 1987,
the labour ward clanked like a cattle-yard,
the same bass moan, the clink and whang of steel,
jealous forceps dangling from spikes,
the rattle of slack pans in the stack,
the tinkle at the tea table, and the telephone
that corralled the clicking heels
and mustered trolleys block to block;
and bed by stainless bed,
sniffing at the sterile linen,
wondering about the stun
the dull-shod men came along the lino line.

ii

A Territory pub was a roof on a fridge,
they drank like every slab was their last:
England was more intimate, a continual sip
of ales and lagers. The oak beams smelt of time,
the conversation of timelessness;
men barracking for broncos and roosters,
eating chicken, talking bullshit
about their father's World War Two,
and making the same low joke
while she's on all fours, squeezing
through a tunnel of pain, crying out:
'Has she had it yet, the old cow?'

iii

Here one bloke braves the ward,
a horizontal shaft into the mountain of life;
stone echoes and walls draped with stained rags;
slaps, cries, shrieks, grapples and in there
someone cuts a belly open,
four gloved hands up to the wrists in blood;
and in there I'm up to my elbow,
tearing the placenta from a fist of muscle;
and in there it sounds like a landing,
nurses hauling bodies up the gory shore,
an unspeakable lagoon
lapping at the doctor's feet.

iv

Like HQ, his wife's room is efficient,
the facilities bare, a clinical ozone, then
as if a button were pushed somewhere else
the midwives bare their teeth and turn with needles
'push, push!' she snarls and the cabinet opens,
the mask falls from the steel cylinder
and in the sulphurous musk of liquor finds
he is clutching the hand of a woman who has gone, gone,
the nurses squabbling like vultures over swabs,
and in a flurry of coverlets and nappies
someone else is breathing and his hands
have no idea what to do.

v

At the pub they told him only watch the women
through a camera, to try for footage of any souls
leaving through the ventilation shafts, but now
the baby has taken his wife's breasts, and her eyes,
they are drained but looking to give more away
and he is searching for a feeling he is supposed to have
but cannot name, and a purpose for the hands
he has pocketed as useless now like his mates
who think they fly with the ball and cannot hear
the crib roll by with its stillborn for dissection
and in a distant cell somebody sobbing
for the blanket snatched as they dreamt away.

vi

His fingers will touch him soon
with the softest skin they can know,
smoother than his life can ever be again,
yes, today his hopeful face is ready
to work the future. In six weeks his kid
will look at him and smile, he'll thrill
to true responsibility, and patience, patience, soon
he will walk back through the caterwauling ward
past the cemetery bleeding from the hospital foundations
hold his child to the winter sun
and feel radiant, immortal,
and suddenly ready to die.

Ultrasound Poem #2

Call them Mum
and Dad:
this unsteady couple
whose knocked-up shack broke
building codes
leaning to the smoky screen.

Plastic gloves and sonic finger
pixel-plunge to grip
the after-image of
their passionate conflagration,
fed an angry timber

that forged this ashen child,
fist waving
from the dying fire
of its creation.

an alternative life

Every moment I am offered an alternative life.
Mostly my task is to stay on course
for that final buoy, out in the endless sea,
that has no known coordinates.
The waves are chaos, shimmering on a spinning globe.
Dependent for my independence,
my life raft's ballasted by documents,
but has no stern, no prow, no tiller;
the only compass in my head.
Bobbing in a huge salt-water basin,
I can't see which way the needle's pointing,
only cross-currents, counter-clockwise,
oscillations, gods, stellar and tidal motion:
one infinite, changeable ocean.

'Imagine the unthinkable'

Imagine the unthinkable?
Don't you write another word.
The economy's unsinkable.

The beer will be undrinkable?
The possibility's absurd.
Why imagine the unthinkable?

The think-tanks too unthinkable:
give up now, follow the herd:
the economy's unsinkable.

The good ship Beer's unsinkable.
It sails the foam, free as a bird.
Imagine the unthinkable?

The concept is undrinkable:
a drunken notion overheard,
the economy's unsinkable

my confidence unshrinkable.
The beer is good, and I have burped.
The economy's unsinkable.
Imagine the unthinkable!

Got a real job

Handed money, handed meaning;
money my anchor, grimly clutched.
Rattle of the chain's receding:
it's cold and I can't see too much.

Perpetual Horoscope

Aquarius

First and foremost today yourself;
last and least your misalignment.
The sun is shining or imagine it is.
It is safe to behave as if you know
something others do not.
Above the clouds the sky is always blue,
the stratosphere ambivalent.
The markets may evaporate:
the cold perfume of petroleum
inhaled by lovers in their automotives.
It could without doubt be you there
kissing in a confined space.

Aries

Today you are conscious, seeking direction
in a directionless environment.
However irrational, continue
the line you are taking, point by point.
Encounter the shimmering sphere,
quantum being, whatever's in your mind.
Learn the surfaces to which you are bound,
the worlds you slip between.
As grain of sand, you grind.
You are friction between two balls of glass.
This history of your progress is opaque,
its principle impenetrable uncertainty.

Cancer

The zodiac is one sign out.
It will come around again.
Some of us should watch for that.
Until then numerals are contestable,
details few, communicants vague.
The moon still drags blood from our bodies.
The lock clicked over is harder to crack.
The ratchets of entropy beguile us.
We wind clocks to tick down.
Others will require you to take action.
Resist their velocity but go along with them.
Accept their co-ordinates for sanity.

Capricorn

Today may be lived on either
side of the Mobius strip, without
beginning or end; the Circle of Perpetuity.
Say it again? You are repeating yourself.
The day is so unwieldy. Break it
up. Cut it with a knife.
The scars of the day intersect with time,
a network to infinity,
beyond and behind even that (words fail).
There's no call to back-pedal;
Even the furthest dimension must return
one to the point.

Gemini

Yearn together, fulfil the unfulfilled.
Stem the youthwards flow of memory.
Gap-toothed Chaos is cackling at disequilibria.
Make two copies of everything, including yourself.
Stabilising disturbances, steady-state wobbling,
elliptical progression, interfering wave forms and vibrations
channelled by magnetic sulci will accentuate
your receptivity to the obvious.
The signs are jiggling about.
There is one interpretation that is definitely for you.
You will read it when you are ready.
Today, a little wariness will not be misplaced.

Leo

Life the inconceivable motion
transfixed to earth, the solar centrifuge,
the crucifixion of inertia.
Nameless, changeless millstone
grinding you to a workable paste of facts,
figures, inexplicable real world concepts;
prone to psychic Doppler shift, static, and
inanimate modulation. A game of rock?
A knob will click and you will be enabled.
Adjust the settings to serenity.
Stretch out with the hours.
Disengage the mechanism.

Libra

Twelve times round to learn you're going round;
twelve more to learn the planets' ellipse;
twelve again to see the stars and twelve at last
to see the graceful infinite twelves.
These years are always beginning,
their momentum irresistible,
the oscillation of history, its symmetrical atrocities:
they puncture faith and deflate transience,
but lifeblood surges synchronous
with the comprehension of plus,
minus, plus, minus. Passive entity, equivocate
before the brashness of decision.

Pisces

Compassionate immobility,
nychthemeral compliance,
squarely afloat the circumstantial ocean:
mind-set carpentry. I see wood,
the tertiary product of galactic tides
too great for us to judge their inclination.
This stillness at the mortal azimuth,
this vertiginous circumorbital synchronicity:
the technicalities are there to confound you.
Learn to work around work, not against it.
Paradox is out to tumble you. Get the insight.
Also, you need a license for solitude. Apply.

Sagittarius

You cannot see, but you can feel, something, you think,
you believe; the mind self-defeating
in its accountancy of being.
The similarities defy the differences and vice versa.
Truth is consciously confabulated:
avoid moral stance, statute and stature.
Angst, ennui and sangfroid
are as devoid of future as the vacuum.
Anxiety accretes semi-precious tomes;
carnivorous spacetime swallows even stars,
emitting just one sine wave in memory, thus
on any graph your survival is an isolated point.

Scorpio

All things retrograde reversed.
Between telescopic proximity and microscopic eternity,
you are suspended in aeons of millennia.
Manipulate the coefficient of attenuation.
Close open gates; open closed gates.
Compensate for ignorance and incapacity.
Confiscate arrogance and stupidity.
TV off. There will be electricity in the air,
your body a spark in the cosmic engine.
The universe once ignited blows apart.
Interaction is strained, then distant, then impossible.
No hope of contact. Reboot yourself.

Taurus

Songs of cores and systems,
hymns of ap- and perihelion,
cataclysmic solar plasma storms!
Collapse into pregnant vacuity.
Fall and continue falling.
The black hole will recreate you.
Subatomic accretion, impetus to matter,
you were broken to be rebuilt.
Almost poetic in intention,
in its irregular lack of reason and rhyme,
trust to encounter the future.
Try to read all the signs.

Virgo

Calculate a radius of benevolence,
the big bang radiation shadow:
an ever-present future,
block and tackle eventuality,
conceptual pulleys, quantum moments…
Belief is a contraction.
You are contracting into yourself.
The shadows of your hands gain focus, losing potential.
Deconstruct, romanticise, reconstruct, resist;
blindly disobedient to an obedient vision,
Keep moving, moving along,
facing the way you are going, singing.

real drone

it is clear right away there is something seriously wrong
the body is lying in the dust and there is blood on the stomach

like a fist plunged in and ripped out a handful of gut
here great vessels are leaking, the blood is filling the belly

if I sear the liver it will cease, we will be able to see again
in the diagram the mesentery looks like America

can we turn down the colour?
click on the fluids icon a couple more times

it's an idealistic simulation
the ideal is what we are fighting for

dust clogs the instruments. the stockmarket's shivering
from lack of blood. you'll be a pilot soon enough

a real drone's harder to control. listen!
the weapons dealer's speaking at the meeting

hours at a screen, are you comfortable there?
you can adjust your seat by pulling on the lever

Two wings make the bird

Another democratic flap –
beaks are sharpened, calls are heard –

the body politic takes off –
on a flight of the absurd –

but ink-dipped wing tips
will write the same word –

Left wing? Right wing?
I'm for the bird.

The solution to us

For Jane

My mathematical love
has two eyes and two feet

her body waves at me
its beautiful equations

subatomic physics spins
my head round, but not hers

always in the same place
black space cold at my back

I orbit around her
steady eye, I am earthed

our lovely universe
the solution to us.

from The Effective Butterfly

The Effective Butterfly

Imagination's fearless wings
brunt the coming storm.

Clouds tower over flooded plains,
millions float face down.

The hurricane's eye
is dry over man.

One butterfly has survived
to circle on a ragged wing.

Its beauty centrifuges a tear
from an orphaned boy.

He stands to watch it pass, and next
the world is lapping at his feet.

An Allemande for Horseback

For Xanthe

Watching me build a yard, for the horses,
you might have argued, crop in hand,
that I had learnt nothing about the animals,
and less about the fence.

I have no strainer for the wire, I have no wire.
Just white electric-fence tape, disconnected,
a single strand to draw the line
the horses usually choose to stay inside.

The bridles, cracked and worn, hang loose
from posts that will rot in three wet years.
If it doesn't rain, I'll hand the paddock back.
If it does, I'm the biodegradable farmer!

The horses are happy where the food is.
They have a clean creek, hills to run free.
Mother and son, they stand muzzle to rump,
let saplings snap in the violent wind.

Grass I picked them cut my fingers,
no good now for the cavalry, my sword hand
slippery with blood. As for love, that's reserved
for the days after they get sugar cubes.

There is what we don't know
and what the horses don't know: for instance
I believe Topaz understands English,
and she believes humans can only see ahead.

I sing them songs to the beat of the hoof.
I sing for all the lucky horses with hills to roam,
with bareback riders, almost lovers,
going at their own pace, hey, slow down Topaz!

I sing for all the horses in confinement,
who died in war, whose riders were ignorant,
whose riders made impolite assumptions,
who beat and swore at them in terror.

I worry about my bones, I need them
for the chain-saw and guitar, I can't afford
another month on the floor. I worry Jim
knows more than he is letting on,

and when the fall comes it is quick and easy,
and my daughter almost topples laughing, and
I laugh too, so that no one says I have learnt nothing
as we ride in silence through the mountains

in the creaking leather saddles, folk singing
in my head, to the hoof beats. The horses like that,
and so long as we go where they want to go,
we all get along at a trot.

Rodent Fugue

Early winter, the jubilant bush flowers, little mammals in the evening.

My hut was warm and smoky, antechinus skipped along the carpentry.
One hundred years of amateurs, the trees kept back the wind.

Creaking like a little wooden ship, I was pacing out my past.
Convict captain's delicacy, nice cut lads!
If my hut was the ship, the rats would quickly jump.

Rats are bastards, they are so like us.
We soil our nest, we sneak along the rigging.
Carpentry and rope, England's Medusas afloat.
Rattus rattus carrying the plague, an ocean of dread.

Crouching in the crow's nest, it's a long way back to England.
Captain Cook my Sisyphus, convicts merely moving stones.
Passengers slipping the purser, like sleek mice.
Myths soak through as sea mist, I'll close the window now.
Two candles is enough to read by, ten would be nice.

Bogong moths, not one of them Icarus.
Moth meat for the moth people, few of whom remain.
My flotsam mattress, rodents scampering on my pillow.
Rodents tug my hairs in sleep, nibble trailing finger-bait.
They have shorted out the tangled twelve-volt system.

I carry water from the creek, in a plastic bucket.
My people must be dreaming, the land is drying up.
The white man's posy florid as a musket shot.
There's trouble with the steerage, his leaking mental boat.

Humans think and think, rodents chew, the oceanic forest waits.
The mice stay timidly on board.
Antechinus tunnel through my hull.

To see the nervous animals, sit quietly and still, remembering the past.
There are many flowers floating in the winter bush.

Silent in my little wooden hut, I close this in my book.

Missa Terra Nullius

Red sky in the morning, smoke in the sky; the animals are anxious.

*

Clouds accumulating like a fugue, are they smoke, are they water?

Hot wind humming the fence lines; a desert plainsong.

*

Stiffening my neck, my hat blows off anyway.

Crescendo-decrescendo, the heavy transports passing.

*

Roses in December, no snow in Old England.

Who would sing against the flowers?

*

The people are many, the people are empty.

The clouds are too high for rain.

*

Our garden is dust, few of us are singing.

We are perfectly evolved for death.

*

Red sky at night, dust in the sky, the sheep-men sigh.

Heat Exhaustion

In the summer of 2006, for eleven anxious days, the Brogo
community was threatened by bushfire.

Soil the colour of home brew, I'm almost there.
I have to rest again, though the gradient is easing up.
From shade to shade, I'm drooping by my bicycle.
I've lots of puff, must be my heart, or hypochondria.

The crisp leaves, the shimmering updraft.
Now I see the enemy, crossing the stony ridge.
He is my age, he too is wilting in the heat.
Sir, I cannot hold the barrel steady.

I'm flat in my scrape like a 'roo.
He's wavering in the hot eucalypt fumes.
The firestorm jets are howling at the land.
The foolish bicycle brigade all falls over.

I could burn amongst the stones and leaves.
Visualise, visualise! Cold beer!
A few metres short of continuity –
slumped before the television, I find out it was 40

Slumped before the television, I find I'm in my forties.
Fears have been renewed, good evening.
Remaining in my house, paying my subscriptions.

The friendly troops have dozers, soldiers on their way.
The infantry is wilting, the desert very hot.
The Arctic is a desert too, the airstrips icing up.

Sweating in Antarctica, what will they think up next?
Cold desensitising, cold sanitising, cold lying.
Yes, but do those on the ground understand the mission?

Reliable, repeatable, indiscriminate parameters.
Seven-point-six-two millimetre, tissue penetration.
The science of ballistics, the psychology of persuasion.

The chaos of the battleground, the smell of shit and diesel.
My helmet's on too tight, but I filled out every form.
There are flaws in the system, I'm in a violent fissure.

The system is aching, there are flaws in my head.
Tightening the definitions, the pressure's on the temples.

Second law of thermodynamics, you are going to sweat.
A rattling cabinet, a violent atmosphere.

Strengthen the interior, it is shrinking from within.
Our riveted intransigence, our fear of losing work.

Shrinking space is heating up, install that air-conditioner.
We've punched a hole in continuity, we hope it fits.

The measurements are not yet right, the contract has them specified.
Cornered worker, the system's squaring up to you.

Fools, we are tightening each other's belts.
The pressure's on the cranium, they have it down to one small pill.

It is a sad world, a happy world, I need my little pill.
Going on and off the pill, your brain will be unsteady.
Bone box, skin wrapping, free death package.
Forty years of television, still there's nothing on.
Free death poses a growing question, the cost of living.
A pill doesn't cost much, I am heating up the atmosphere.
Can the helicopters put it out, my burning life?

Thrum of choppers ten ks north, better get some beer in.
The bush doesn't mind a fire, but we do.
It's a section 44, the agencies co-perate – it must be bad.
Birds fly off, bulls and wombats dip their brows.
No one wants to hear the horses screaming.

We'll fight it on our bicycles, you're pedalling insanity!
Individuals dysfunctional, they freak or knuckle under.
Humidity and smoke, the ash could seed the paddocks.
The drought must break, but by whose command?
Clouds of ash won't rain, but don't call off the dancing.

Scarce uniforms of Reason, but humans form their front.
Belly crawling house to house, installing happy endings.
We beat the other species, it was our long-term plan.
The dozer crews doze, soil the colour of home brew.
After rain a darker ale, frog spawn froth on the dam.

When I'm Cleaning Windows

Detergent feathers the window, my hand flies around.
The birds are watching, I hate to do it to them.

When I'm Cleaning Windows, I think but do not whistle.
George's ukulele picked some funny little ditties.

'Leaning on a lamp-post', many couples doubled over.
Their childhood was in wartime, their windows blacked out.

Yorkshire swirled in coal dust, anyone could see the smut.
The pits were blackest windows, canaries whistled underground.

Yorkshire pudding, railway pudding, rhubarb, onion, spud.
White legs in the bathtub, Formby's audience giggling upstairs.

My relatives were window-cleaning, seeing their reflection.
I see me too, but also them, their passing by.

I feed the birds, it doesn't help them see the glass.
I let the windows dirty, until the fledglings learn.

I can see them waiting now, in the stricken trees.
Each year necks are broken, on the window-panes.

Lying limp in my hand, a bird is mostly feathers.
I can hold its beauty, only now it's flown.

from **Flying Doctor**

I am singing and dreaming
in my poor way
over the earth
– Chippewa Amerindian Shaman fragment

4. Flying Doctor

When the bush pilot first off drops the brake so hard
his prop spits dirt from the strip, you feel glad
you have a government pilot with a Nomad,
though the oxygen cylinder clunks in the nose cone
and you are not too sure of your self.

Someone had to do it, people are hard to find,
I only did it for a few months, it's just a taxi
by air instead of by road, let's demystify this thing,
I had a nurse, a list of patients, and a taipan
circling the clinic, like a salesman with its poison.

I was there in person, the fearless flying shaman,
realised from the belly of the craft,
and when I flew in, the glib rivers flickered
like dreamtime snakes, they vanished
towards the central desert,

and I crossed the coastlines and the ocean
and the boundaries of language
in my magical machine, and with my helpers
I flew in the cures to all the illness
that my people sent in there before me.

Thinking about Wang Wei,

one spring evening in the Brogo, after a visit from Ouyang Yu

Like Wang Wei I am a crazy poet living far upstream,
drinking and letting the moon light my room.

Like Wang Wei I listen to the bush at night.
I fear the silence no more than he did.

Like Wang Wei I cannot count the stars,
but I would know the name of each.

Like Wang Wei I sing the choir of frogs.
Ten thousand voices bubble, bubble.

Like Wang Wei I think one should concentrate on non-being.
Laughing, I try to neutralise my years of understanding.

Like Wang Wei I ask my friends the birds,
can human-being and not-being truly share my head?

I don't know about Wang Wei, but I have Jane,
and all the cold night she sleeps through my questions.

Letter to T'ao Chien

Full moon, it's been about ten thousand years,
and distant dogs still bark, T'ao Chien.

They will not leave me alone.
I follow the Way and it follows me.

Dark cloud-bars cross the chance of light.
In a sullen wind, trees keep their heads down.

Too many dogs, too many people, too much noise;
and all that they have done since you left T'ao Chien

is turn my clay cup to a glass,
into which I pour the same old questions.

I sip the answering wine by the fire
when cloud and wind have left together.

Crossing the street, avoiding a roasting

Electric-Zephyr curling wand:
day-long the hot wind
rolled the raffle tickets.

Then the sun dropped
like a gold coin donation
from a blue rinse sky.

When it thumped the velvet, two Army
ladies at the playing table looked up
with gracious wrinkled smiles.

It's an Australian salvation,
passing by, reaching a salaried hand
into an agnostic pocket.

Making Soap

for Mollie

Making soap my favourite job, time just slipped away.
In the open paddock, a world as obvious as that.

The lonely tree would often drop another stick.
I threw it, Mollie fetched and panted at my feet.

She tried to trip me with it, she did, sometimes!
The little puffs of dust settled on our toes.

Scrubbing plastic moulds in plastic tubs, I was content.
Nothing shattered in the sink, if it fell I'd pick it up.

I know I chipped our wedding bowl, but my hands were trembling.
The soap made it slippery, I lost my grip back then.

One soapy mouthful as a child, I took more care with swearing!
Good clean discipline, I don't remember what the word was.

Now I was making soap to wash the dirt from town.
Adding Brogo essence, a swirl of stick and sky.

Water, caustic soda (gloves and glasses), olive oil.
A home-made stirrer, dinkum Aussie metal.

The dog just wouldn't rest. Mollie! Sit!
My two minds spun like a twin-tub washer.

The mixture loses clarity, the hours go twirling by.
The flashbacks too were fading, the sun stayed on the rails.

The intubated woman, her wrists tied to the bed.
The hospital smell, chlorhexidine and latex.

My soap was too gentle for hospital shrouds.
In the living paddock I sniffed the obvious world.

I needed washing, a dirty soapmaker!
It was drought time, I didn't shower for days.

A dry excuse, solitude.
The stick did not disturb the sky.

The giant tree was strong for both of us.
It had a possum to scratch its itching bark.

Parrots hung like bangles from its many arms.
An eternal dog chased an eternal stick around its base.

Chenrezi, God of one thousand hands, in every palm an eye.
And every eye compassionate, blinking like our lives.

As Mollie's paws brushed past, the grass would bow down.
'Excuse me,' it would whisper, 'we are blessed.'

And I would lean back over the tub.
And the tree was profligate with its shade.

An Unseen Wind

For a moment the dark water is quiet, so that the white gull of understanding can easily find its way to the island where there is a hut, a desk, and a book, and on the open page a haiku, my favourite poem, by Matsuo Basho: 'The sea dark / the call of the teal / dimly white'.

The sea may be quiet but it is never really still, even if the waves, from time to time, cancel each other out, at other times they will amplify each other, and even if there were no waves the sea itself would be one great wave, dragged like a veil across the face of the earth by that stony-faced bride the moon.

On the ocean nothing is nothing, motion is never absent, and the bird is alive, and like Matsuo's haiku, insignificant against the cosmos, one tiny poem, the bird flying across the vast watery abyss, the speck of white barely seen against the seething grey, so that from a boat it would be difficult to make out as it emerged from the horizon of nothing and dissolved back into that vague dimension, the binoculars tiring to hold, and the waves knock-knocking at the boat's door that if opened would sink us utterly.

Li Ching Chao, ancient poetess in your silken robe, we have missed you for nine hundred years, I would show you to my wooden boat, but 'Who can take a letter beyond the clouds?' you might ask, and answer right away 'Only the wild geese come back and write their ideograms on the sky', and so we are agreed a poem is a bird, and I can ready my boat to launch into Bashō's vast haiku, the silken leash straining tense at the island pier, but all of a sudden we feel it is pointless now to speak, how would the bird or the ocean know how lonely it can be, so I pull back in my ridiculous canoe, and its bamboo sail breaks up and floats away, the moment cast in hexagrams, now the yielding, now the abysmal, a curtain of fate, opening on those days when I was young that would seem to last forever, but now, as I urge myself to record them, in my hut the full moon floods the room and my desk so that the sheet of paper I unsheathed is momentarily lost in the white light.

The gull is alone against a backdrop of immeasurable ocean, now a dim white speck on the murmuring darkness, now lost altogether in choppy conditions, now clearly discernible again, a lone bird brought by the poet into weightless balance with the mass of the world, life poised as a shining point above the infinite unknowing void, the teal of life, the ocean of death, the self against the ocean of human consciousness, Bashō has brought the momentous and the insignificant into an equal relation, a bird and a planet into perfect balance.

The call of the teal is the line to the future, the bird follows its own voice, its wings can be heard beating the invisible air, the teal is there, calling now, I know it is alive over the endless water, making its unhurried but inexorable way to the land we cannot see but know is there over the edge of the page, the land that restrains this ocean's infinity, the shore that measures the sound of the waves, the pacific boundary of certainty the bird is always nearing, its ambassadorial call, but to whose nation could it be calling, or what isolated cry is this, and what has a bird to do with the thoughts of man, and how does its call float like this over the sea of the page, the wave-crest lines, my pen's tip now flying out across the wilderness of water, in blind need like the teal, a need it has the call for, a need to calm the ocean, to demonstrate the impossible, to exist alone but as one of many drawing life across the abyss, the eternal migration of living across a blank universe, asking with the voice of Rumi 'How can anyone say what happens, even if each of us dips a pen a hundred million times into ink?', his lines rippling away, my ink salt-water, like tears, for now the dark sea is time, the teal the second hand, running smoothly down its face.

I am the bird, the tear, the blemish on the dark face of perfection, caught in place, though everything is moving, though its time runs out like a line as it carries us across the water, wings shaping the waves in air, everything timed, moving to its own rhythm, wave-rise and fall complex past predictability, the simple beat generating precious complexity, whose price is chaos, a numerological cloud obscuring the view of the true one-zero universe of Zen, upon which we meditate but which is terrifying should we glimpse it, that infinite, boundless space it is better for the bird not to think about, that absolute lack of direction that must never be allowed to distract its migration, our time reduced to that line, our limited protection.

The character of the bird is arrow, it is 'get to the point', the straight line to the vicious beak, sharp radius of fear sweeping up the circle, a point and a line, a zero and a one, a dimension too bleak and daunting for life, a notion Matsuo must acknowledge but then try to dodge, Zen monk caught in bow fight, the arrow heading directly for its target, the centre of one, the fearful zero, the death of a life without complexity, without the human poem, at least one haiku, three lines, five, seven and five syllables, piercing the yes no binary to open up to us the prime universe creating life, the planetary forces lifting and illuminating the white point against the great darkness, for at this moment neither the bird nor the sea moves, life the inevitable motion is the unseen energy that keeps the haiku working its powerful wings, flying steadily through time and space contained.

It is life versus death, the black and the white, thought versus what, we behave as if we believe in absolutes when really we don't, so let's not, we can't, life can't, because if the bird was purely white and the ocean purely black there would be a white hole in a black sheet, one star only, a dead pixel on a screen, so the bird and the ocean must take their imprecise relation from each other, and we must cling to the falseness of certainty like the fuzz on the planet itself, our biosphere rich in the DNA that Bashō never intended should be reduced to one bird hoping for land and carrying with it nothing.

The sea is dark but I can make the bird out, so there must be light, but Bashō would not forget the moon if it was up, and the bird, though white, could not light the whole scene, so this must be an in-between time, the sun's light diffusing across the ocean, too bright for me to see the other stars, compass fires in the dark, fires oblivious to the wind that I feel blowing, the heartless wind that casts cold terror, plummeting us like stones in black water.

In terror we lose our way, why explain, that question again and again, where are we, where is the end, do you see the gull from the side, or from above, so small, so small it is almost nothing, almost flipping into the negative, that raven crossing the white noise of my mind, the haiku dropped and fluttering down towards the churning white and almost being lost, but for the merciful hand of Bashō catching it just above the pond, and for the frog watching from a favourite wet rock.

I take the poem and I float it in the bowl of my mind, letting Bashō go back to getting pissed on home-brew sake with his friends, his words carrying them away, far from the poem, his hand like a teal, waving to Retznikoff writing 'If only I could write with four pens between five fingers/ and with each pen a different sentence at the same time', and his compassion which in human hands is only love, his haiku's crystalline drops that gather to an ocean, the teal's pure note simple as the emptiness it fills, a straight-forward assertion of existence, inaudible to those too complex for simplicity, for one pond, one rock, one frog.

Bashō's friends sat there in peace, and the bird flew past, and their mouths fell open, and if they had no pen and paper what sort of haiku poets would they be, Bashō asked the cautious novice with the pale hands, who asked where could a haiku fly to, and why could the ocean not be a sake-soaked mat and the bird the white thread, stitches wing-beats, a living machine, squadrons of machines, all independent but all working together to sew the ocean to the land, and so Bashō reminded them all the page once had been a tree the bird sang in, and it is child's play for haiku to tear the page from the book and to make an origami bird, because thankfully humour survives even though it must swim with destruction, with the oceanic potential of ink, with fish like thoughts running beneath the surface, with the oceanic potential for life, the lines the poem draws as coast, and waves, and the parallels one could infinitely draw, the ripples in space-time, fish-thoughts breaking the surface, the hungry gull's eye seeking the poem.

Playing yin-yang by the goldfish pond, the game of Go-Haiku, Bashō has placed the first stone, it is tiny but it is equal to the ocean, oh how they need each other, and though it changes everything the next move comes, like the next beat of the wings, and 'I am a scribbled form, drawn with a pen, upon a parchment,' King John proclaims, 'and against this fire, I shrivel up', and even an ocean becalmed cannot hold the game, or dampen Shakespeare's fire, and so the bird flies on, to the land there must be beyond our restless imagination.

What can the teal know of this world too hard to define, where the poem is a perfect pebble, the white stone of Revelation, 'and in the stone a new name written, which no man knoweth saveth he that receiveth it', a syllable cupped in a compassionate hand, the clear water in the blue lagoon of mind, my ego the gull floating serenely over the ocean, my id breaking softly on the reef, my superego poem asking what can I know about being the bird, I am not its observer, its watcher who makes it real, merely one who hears the observer's call, feels his fatigue, his distance, the watcher of the watcher of the poem of myself, migrating across the great birth-to-now sea of understanding, a sea into which I inscribe myself, a salted droplet, a feather, a stone, an unseen wind, a suffusing light, a receptacle for love, for compassion, the water closing over my words and washing the ink away, the dim white gull receding, calling I…I…I…

Then somewhere on the ocean's rippling face my image reappears, it forms and dissolves, forms and dissolves, and I am flickering forever across the surface of the blue planet, smiling into space, beckoning the lovers to come in their boats, to sail our Aegean of the Sagittarian Arm, to watch our bird flying on ahead, to land on worlds I have neither time nor space to tell.

Bega: slipping through

Sometimes there is snow on the Brown,
ice on Big Jack, so we take the
Tantawangalo road, crunching gravel
above the huge mossy boulders of the creek.
Or we come down on bitumen from the north,
through Cooper's Gully where icicles hang
from deciduous limbs, and water-licensees
sow purple circles: picnic-skirts of frost
spread on the yellowing grass. Clouds of whey
like puffs of smoke from a cheese train
lumber over paddocks near the factory,
the damp morning air holding them down
to the creek flats like doonas on well-made beds.
Town is all the bedside tables clumped together
after the milk and money flood. Main street is
a showy coverlet, never quite in harmony
with the season, because business is in a shabby office
out the back, over the account books,
and the city is pouring in to town,
everybody asking 'Who is that? Where do you suppose
she got that dress?' and saying to each other
'I think I'll get a pair of those sunglasses.
My phone is humming. "Hello?"'
I told them I would leave
when the traffic lights arrived.
Now there are four sets in the shire,
I strongly prefer the green.
Orange is OK, so long as there is time.

Red? I can see one day
I won't mind a rest on the long drive in,
but right now I'm on my way home from work,
and I still like to slip through
when I think no one is looking.

Shakespeare in Newcastle

Shall I compare thee to a summer's day?
(No Through Road. Keep Dogs on Leash)
Thou art more lovely and more temperate:
(Turn Left onto Service Road)
Rough winds do shake the Darling Buds of May,
(Please Bathe between the Flags)
And summer's lease hath all too short a date:
(For Sale)
Sometime too hot the eye of heaven shines,
(Sinners can Never be Winners)
And often is his gold complexion dimmed;
(Closed on Sundays)
And every fair sometime from fair declines,
(Merging Traffic)
By chance or nature's changing course untrimm'ed;
(Roadworks. Slow Down)
But thy eternal summer shall not fade,
(Last Year's Prices!)
Nor lose possession of that fair thou owest;
(Underground Parking)
Nor shall Death brag thou wander'st in his shade,
(Wrong way. Go back.)
When in eternal lines to time thou grow'st:
(Queue here for tickets)
So long as men can breathe or eyes can see,
(Pedestrian Crossing)
So long lives this, and this gives life to thee.
(No Stopping on Freeway)

Recession to a point

In the end there was only one job left.
20 million applicants joined the queue,
which went right around Australia
in a perfectly leaderless circle,
each person asking the one before
'What should I put on my CV?'
'Who is running this show?'
'What should I wear to the interview?'
'What is the job, anyway?'
'Perhaps if there is only one job,
it is being Jesus' suggested one.
'Well that stuffs my chances,' said the next,
'I'm off to grow vegetables to sell
to the people in the queue' and at that
our strung-out nation broke up
into little knots of people,
and the conversation was eager and
went far into the star-clear night.

The beer lover's funeral

Life, mate, is obvious enough when the baby gets bored,
and the toddler plays lion in the rickety jungle of chairs,

and life is the priest in white, and Janet whom you never met
reading from the scriptures in a clear and present voice,

and life is the red fire extinguisher beside the door
the no-smoking sign above the toilet

the boys of the brigade seated in sober blue
the ceiling fans going round and round

and the great mass of sorrowful air
moving down the hall, out the doors

past the sausage sizzle and into the cicada's haze.
And like a bush poem without a rhyme there was

a sense of disappointment too – imagine, mate! –
no bloody beer at a boozers do!

from **Red Song of the Red Earth**

A Rose Asunder

a poem   written each day to its destination   isn't you but your
madness – Yang Lian

I

A hot day under my hat.
38 degrees of accumulated significance
and the roses wilt,
each petal a theory now lapsed.

Dishevelled briar
exhaust has smudged your face.
He had his indicator on
but drove straight through.

Flouncing by the roadside,
draped across the brickwork
you relish the secateurs,
and the lesser flowers' cringing.

You do not care which way he turns
at your crucial roundabout.

II

The flowers are out, but the people are in.
In their houses, in their cars.
In their heads. Sunglassed eyes
fed polarised light. Who's there?

Primaries at the plastic children playground.
The prefab lawn is saving energy
by not producing oxygen.
Colour is vibrant, and deceased.

Let's go shopping in the mall,
where the air conditioner hums to itself –
a smug little tune about a heatwave.
Let's get a shiny steel shower-rose.

Unwrap the geranium soap.
Smell the crushed flowers.

III

The roses spit
like six-inch guns.
Even peaceful folk
want to pluck them.

The front yard swivels
like a weapons platform
from which a mouth
snaps 'chatter chatter'.

Everybody's in the wrong.
The line to the spouse
is a long slow fuse
but one day, I tell you…

Cross the street and watch the roses
don't cough up cups of blood.

IV

(Einar Wry-Mouth, Earl of Orkney, d. AD 1020)

The rose of the throat
in its blue vein vessel
swells with the lustful dream
of my enemy's mortal scream.

This Norseman strides impatient
for the sword-thrust, the gargling lung,
the runnel-blood. For the moaning head
to breathe its last on his weary thigh.

We might have lived together
where sheep scratch their briskets
on standing stones. Now I must pen
my warrior poem with this sword.

I shall take your woman
when you have burned at sea.

V

Twelve roses like a jury
ate my equanimity for lunch.
One was an unyielding white.
Two fake blonde. Three had noses pink

from running in the snow. The rest?
Redheads. My bank account lay supplicant.
The barrister brought me coffee smothered
with a love heart made of froth.

In every plush chamber
of my heart the gavel fell.
The sentence arrested me.
What I thought was love was only money.

I read all the poets, but
they could not prevent my life.

Red Song of the Red Earth

'The Song of Grief shall sound, laughing, in your soul' – Mahler:
The Song of the Earth (trans. various)

Burling down the Stuart Highway! Flying along!
The sky is blue forever, and the Earth stands firm:
like a new bull-bar, an oxyacetylene weld
from a gin-drinkers rusting backyard shed.
The Song of the Earth, I have it trapped, hammering
against the windows of the car, trumpet notes
like blowfly nuggets ricocheting, then
battered corrugated iron flapping out
a desert chorus. A distant crowbar is heard
rupturing a chemical drum; Mahler's frustrated fists
beat against walls of tin; there is the neigh
of an anxious horse outdoors. A concluding thud lacerates
an alcoholic's leathery scalp.
My heart is weary…I weep alone.
At Wycliffe Well they feel this too, and therefore
have invited the aliens to land and keep them company.
Model 'Greys', fibreglass extraterrestrials, clothed
in safety-vest fluorescent green, stand casually about
this leyline intersection guarded by the unnerving traffic lights
of Korsakoff's psychosis, where out the corner
of a demented old bastard's eyes (two devil's marbles,
in direct alignment with the mob up north)
flying saucers smash at light speed against the mongrel chef's
splashboard. Who knows where anyone round here really comes
    from?

At the petrol pumps, the uncertain smiles of caravanners, our own
soft grey nomads who quickly look away. They fill their tanks
and order hamburgers with the lot. The cost of everything
is high, and reality reminds them of a documentary they saw
 back east.
Some clicks north a spinifex pigeon died on their windshield.
An identified flying object, disoriented, its mission a mystery
and abruptly terminated. Or perhaps that was the mission? A
 message
meaning what? Assuming the wishbone split on impact,
I wish for all things to be connected.
The bridge stands like a half-moon that could evolve
in either direction, but the young men have stopped looking
 from it
to the horizon. They are staring down dejected at the creek of stone,
drinking away their rec leave from the entrenched battalions of
 Ali Curung.
What normally flows over the bridge is beer, in the trucks that
 carry it.
There is nothing to do. World-war work digging wolframite at
 Wauchope
died decades ago. The strangely soft mineral is left in the ground,
 that once
was turned to tungsten carbide, tipping armour-piercing munitions,
cutting through iron like a bull-bar through the wildlife.

A truckie relaxes into the steel railings, draws on a cigarette, and
    knocks some pelt
from the metal. He eyes the boys on the bridge, smiles privately
    at a joke.
They are laughing now, but will one of them jump tonight?
Or select a road-train to cut and paste himself into the next
    dimension,
a human slash-and-burn operation to wring the water
from a mother's eyes? All wet and puffy. Nothing here
makes the city papers, though there is
in the flash of her eyes...the agitation of her heart
a great red dust storm from the Tanami that makes you think
you really are on angry Mars this time, and then the floodwaters
    spring
from the left of nowhere. Windows wound up, I did not hear
the thunder
over Mahler, who is one of those big German guns

from so many years ago they seem romantic now.
The bridge's arch is inverted and thus completes a circle
that floats on the earth submerged. Reflected as well, the blue
    sky lies
at our feet. It surrounds us now, we could vanish into it, alien
wormhole theory, sucked in by our own misconception, while
    the earth
quietly inhales the water into its fractured aquifer, its bedrock lung.
While it is waiting, the road takes a snooze, awash
with fossil-fuel dreamings beneath its sodden doona.
What do I hear when I awake? A bird singing in the tree.

Fair assumption that's what it is. Why on Earth
would aliens choose here to land? Desolation's beach-head!
Endless red sand, the blue ocean drained away aeons back.
Here the imagination struggles to lift off, up and away
from the stubbies in the dust, the shattered glass like stars
that salt the soil with crystals of trapped and disappointed light.
Scalp-blood is the sign of hope draining away, and yet,
just as well, the confirmation of our resilient nature,
reinvigorated every time we wake.
I can drive right past at one hundred and thirty, leave this place
to siphon out the rear-view mirror but I don't.
I pull over for a deep breath from the vastness.
There is interstellar dust too: it blocks the light calling
from all those lonely stars. Our problems can be solved, we tell
 ourselves.
This is an injured surface. It is the fantasy we clutch,
when we stop to stretch our legs on it, to drink the silence
of the endless road, that despite our homeless wandering,
and every day the sun falling and the sky showing its wound,
we are needed wherever we may be;
and that no matter what we do to each other, each night
the Earth breathes, deep in peace and sleep.

The Desert

for Ian McFarlane, author and critic

That spinifex that tumbles across the red hot sands
in those windy poems of the desert
is not spinifex. Spinifex is glued to the ground.
That poor lonely beautiful mountain duck
with a sad limp and a broken wing
is making it up; leading you away from its brood.
That possum is not the feral animal: your bloody cat is,
and that cute koala will rip your face if you get too close.
And philosophy's egg, deceptively unblemished, lies
nestled in the cribs of vanquished skulls.

Of all people the bloody poets
should get it right, or they will stuff our metaphors
right up, mate. Whoever said a day trip
gave them the right to speak on season?
They should check their facts, brush up
on John Clare, the middle T'ang, and Shaw Neilson.
To name a few.

If you get off the train and walk
you will soon toughen up. The boxthorn
will teach you about long pants and boots.
You will want to buy a gun
to shoot then eat that bloody duck.
The koala has its back turned on the desert
and munches mountain leaves. No cat would care.

Don't believe what poets say about death.
They drink too much; they are pathological livers.
What the fuck would they know?
See those blokes who really know the land?
Are they talking?

The desert, drip-fed with tears of frustration,
waits to teem again with life.
The land is drunk dry by feral cattle,
deer, camels, goats, pigs, rabbits, cats,
donkeys, dogs, farmers and tourists.
The desert is not always a desert,
or a metaphor. There are tasty ducks. Braces of quail,
budgerigar. Delicate portions of crab, lizard, fish.
Mostly though it is hot shards of quartz,
bull spinifex spines, a throat in need of beer.
It cracks that philosopher's egg wide open
to let in the silence and the light.

Poetry's a desert. There are days
it wants to kill you.

Rare Dog Salad

I'm grateful you're a rarity, in a town of dogs,
you canine psychopath with weird green eyes:
rabid pools of algal slime encircled
by your off-white plastic muzzle-bucket;
you petrol sniffer-dog splashing through
the rainbow oil-on-water slick
that darkly wets the concrete apron
of this night-time petro-kennel.

Something's cooking in the fumes, your sodden tail
slips and snakes like a fibbing job description
for a diesel-powered kitchen-hand
frying burger meat for wide-eyed travellers
translocated from some disturbing city
of the leaded mind, their inexorable hunger
like the timeless wind that levels the stone heart
of the ancient hills whose rock cracks in the heat,
then tumbles through the spinifex to never rise again.

Veins of quartz, white shadows of the eucalypts,
drool like crusted dribble from the corner of
an old old mouth that's fast asleep. The clumping grass
is brushed by breeze but is, deep down, set
stubble-straight like a pelt in permanent fright.
Corellas squawk and turn like a crowd
in patent leather shoes on the dance floor
of the gallery of cloud-on-wheels that rumbles over
abandoned mines out west: Black Angel,
White Devil, along the Warrego road.

Lightning wipes the scene but I keep walking,
the report on Eskimos in childbirth, secured
by just a paperclip, tucked underneath
a sweating arm. A yelp signifies singeing skin:
oil boiling hot from a quick-flipped rissole
frizzling. A surface phenomenon. Walking on,
electrocardiographic dots discarded
spot the dust like a bad painting by that sick old man
who used his last breath to abscond again,
or like raindrops on a hospital bandage, spattered,
ochre-stained, frayed like the bitumen's edge.

It's hard to believe the rabies virus lies
dormant on some island to the north.
I hope someone is testing for it. This town
is barking mad, but not that mad:
it's the humidity, and the heat.
And while I've got your ear, I reckon someone
should ask the old man who owns the dog.

from The Underwritten Plain

from To the reader

The poem is set at the Albala-Karoo bore, which today is nothing more than a hole cut in the Nullarbor plain.

One rusted strand of wire hopefully suffices to warn the passer by. Nearby are some abandoned yards, an old highways water-tank, and a headstone for one Herman Johnson. In 1992 an optical fibre cable was laid alongside. No one has lived here for a long time, and visitors are few.

The site is in South Australia, about 60 kilometres ENE of Eucla, along the old highway surveyed in the late 1800s by Ernest Giles and others. The limestone plain, known as Karst from the type site in Czechoslovakia, is undercut with a largely unmapped cave system. The Aboriginal people believed that the great creation snake, locally called Wonambi, moved through the desert using these conduits. The cool air blast from these caves and natural vents in the plain on the hottest of days was Wonambi's breath. The nearby Koonalda cave contains some intriguing diagrams dated at 22,000 years.

Here at the southern limit of the Nullarbor, Australia ends in high cliffs, dropping down for a hundred metres to form the clean curve of the Great Australian Bight. The poem begins imagining the first person to ever see this abrupt and spectacular end to the vast stone slab that is our continent.

from Part I

Mirning know the stories, Mirning speak the dreaming.
Wongai tell their stories the right way.

But hey what's this? We need a story here!
Kangaroo's journey finished here!

Wombat was turned back here!
Dingo could not run around this place!

Like ants at the waterhole's edge, we cannot see across.
It smells of salt and the sound of thunder does not end.

Wonambi lives down those holes.
Have Mirning found his secret home?

Mirning will find the names for this place.
Mirning will find the way to the water.

At Koonalda our fathers went down.
Into the earth, they went down to meet the snake.

Moon-man did not follow them to light their way.
In the snake's breath, the torch burnt down too fast.

They left some signs, but not their meaning.
They sprayed some ochre, but could not see their hands.

They said they did not meet Wonambi.
They said they felt its chill breath closer.

They left us after that, to follow Emu's track.
My father's father left with them, to find the right story.

I tell the stories they left with us.
I cannot tell those they took away.

Wonambi showed the water where to flow.
Our elders followed on their journey.

Here it tunnelled underground,
swallowing Mirning, swallowing stories.

Our wise men given stories in return –
we must protect them.

Our women given children in return –
we must protect them.

Black hole, white ochre.
Here we sit and sing.

And when the song falls away
we breathe in, and start again.

The ones who are lost are returned to us,
through the blood-fringed passage of woman.

I wonder, did Wonambi take my father?
Was it the snake that swallowed his stories?

It threw his white bones back up.
Strewed them around its hole.

Bats are the blowing ashes
of the words he left us.

When the snake's tail flicks
I jump out of the way!

It flicks and vanishes up
into that big hole in the stars.

from Part II

Let's make a note here, right away.
I'm not the poet of the day.

I'm just a poet of the plain.
To lit'rature my work's no gain

and out here I can plainly see
my audience comprises me.

One couplet short of a sonnet?
Let's not extemporise upon it.

If in error I steal a rhyme
well honestly I thought it mine.

My name will never grace a shelf
so I can write to please myself.

Out here to meet myself at last.
Myself, away from all my past.

Yet my head swarms with old stories.
Foolish ones. No wars, no glories.

Is it madness to name each tree
after people dear to me?

My friends who yearned to roam so free?
My friends who helped me cross the sea.

I ran away from wedding cake.
I fled for sweet Mathilda's sake.

No one will ever find me here.
I can relax. Dismiss my fear.

I talk with birds, like St Francis
but with snakes I take no chances.

Human beings I think worse snakes
than the black's Wonambi, who makes

them jittery. When we came through
with sheep that time, then the bore crew –

no surprise they met us with spears.
But they soon overcame their fears.

Next, camel breath, tetchy horse, sweat-
soaked saddle-blankets. And remorse.

The iron horse will ride this plain,
and they'll have learnt to ride in vain.

'Ark ark' the ravens near and far
are curious but wary.

They know that sometime I will die,
and my gun's no longer scary.

I have made small report. This land
has drained my pen and stilled my hand.

It hasn't rained, and never yet
did it – t'was only drops of sweat

that I felt falling from the brim
of my hat, flung now to the wind

across the plain, a scrap of bark.
I ride. The raven's crow 'ark ark'.

from Part III

It's only yards and a bore, mate.
Albala-Karoo. What does that mean?

I dunno. Bloody hole in the bloody ground.
Why don't you ask your cousin?

Who's my cousin!?
Fire up the digger, mate.

Mate, it's a heritage site.
Bullshit.

And obviously sacred.
Mate, look around. No one gives a shit.

Treat it with respect mate.
Yeah yeah. OK.

Yeah the bore hole breathes,
same as the caves mate.

It's the temperature gradient.
Cool, eh?

Love my traditional air conditioning?
Problem is, you have to stand just here.

So, in the mind of early man
it could have been down there –

a cold-blooded reptile –
the dreamtime snake Wonambi?

Plenty of caves to hide in.
Keeping his head down, since Maralinga, mate.

What kind of white man would stay here
long enough to die?

The barbed wire has torn his story to shreds.
What this nail held fast is lost.

Oh spare us the poetry, mate, it's hot today.
How do you know he was a white man?

Was he some kind of spirit being
to the Mirning? Good, or bad?

Good. Otherwise he would not have survived here.
Mate, he didn't survive here.

(At night the dingoes recall
a disquieting sense of loss.)

Old Herman will be busy, now we have laid
our cable to rest beside him.

Fibre optic cable, coast to coast!
'From the cable to the grave'…

'Ark ark' as the ravens say,
killer humour, mate.

Day and night millions of words
will flow past his underground ear

Yeah yeah, what's the marker number, mate?
2.7.6. underground river of light.

Poor Herman! He will be tormented
by all the babble he came here to escape.

from Part IV

Black hole,
inkwell.

I dip my finger
into ancient

memory
oldest mind

make a circle
in the sand.

Red grains
make way

for beginning
and end.

Dark well,
gravitational lens

for examining in depth
my fear. My deepest origin.

For magnifying
my loneliness.

Pinned already
to be dragged

to be spiralling in
to be holding my breath

hoping I will be spat out
on this side of the world.

Black hole
in the land.

Black hole
in the sky.

The first
is air

the second
dust.

In my head, in my eyes –
twin black holes reflect, reflect

yet consciousness
somehow exists.

My black hole
is imperfect

information
is emerging.

Bats flitter out
like useless facts.

Insects are walking
up and down the walls.

Birds nest on
undercut shelving.

My metaphor generator
has audible ball bearings.

Moon was a man
chasing women.

Women were stars
running away.

Sometimes they tripped
and fell to earth.

Loud noise
when they hit the ground!

Maybe they wormed their way
deep underground

leaving us a hole
to skirt.

Worldwide, people left the caves
a long time back.

We are still painting
our fear on the walls

of great galleries, ours
in blazing light

and from the greatest light
the galactic core's black hole

the masterful vortex
is still dragging us

helpless against the infinite
back to ourselves.

Eerie pink, pre-dawn.
A weird mist.

Dingo calls
slip through.

One day's walk
from the southern ocean.

The dew so heavy
it can be drunk from leaves.

Sipping light
with water:

two ways to refresh
your waking thirst.

from **Numbugga Dumb Bugger**

Karma Farmer

freely, to the tune of 'Gods on our Side' by Bob Dylan

Oh I was Buddhist, and I moved to the bush.
The city was noisome, I needed some 'shoosh'.
But I murdered six stink bugs, squashed under my tyre:
the estate agent saw this, and pushed the price higher.

He said 'You're no farmer' as I fumbled the gate.
'I care for my Karma, for that is my fate.'
'I'd care for those chickens, if I was you love.
He'll wait for good fencing, old Buddha above.'

'Oh he's not above' I explained, 'nor a he.
He's all around us, both you and both me.'
'Like blowflies in summer from the dags on your sheep
or the mossies at night-time when I'm trying to sleep.'

Well my house was a beauty, but I stayed outside her
For there in the door frame lived a sentient spider.
My first night was chilly, out there in the shed,
And the fur-coated possums brawled over my head.

I rang my little bell and took to bare feet.
I gazed at still water, so illusory.
But just near Nirvana old biology
filled up my bladder so I had to pee.

Well my second morning it came and it went,
but then came the night-time with my non-self again.
I tried to meditate, but my karmic mind
would not be deterred from thoughts quite unkind.

For the chickens betrayed me, I was cruelly misled.
I paid for chook pellets: they ate beetles instead.
I prayed for the souls of the insect departed
and the E coli killed each time that I farted.

Next my dear Buddhist pussy dragged home a pigeon.
I screamed 'That's that!' and changed my religion.
No more meditating, no more lentils to bake.
I prayed that that agent would choke on his steak.

'Oh my Karma's all used up, I'm Catholic again.
I know you'll forgive me, for the devil's my friend.'
That's what I said to that man on the phone.
'Come out here for dinner, I'm here all alone.'

I loaded a calf up and started the car.
'You never paid rent now it's the abattoir.
That man's the real devil we have to surmount.
Curse my Buddhist detachment from my bank account.'

Well that is my story though I know there's no me.
There's no agent either: he choked on his tea.
I work in my garden, the compost I turn,
and sometimes I spy him returned as a worm.

I'm still out at Wyndham, just me and my gun.
Religious salesman are the ones that I shun.
For I've got my own agent, who spares me the toil
of reading the scriptures for he's there in my soil.

Revenge it can eat you, or so I have heard,
but when I see a worm, I whistle for birds.
I find that amusing, as the years go by
and I love squashing stink-bugs that fall on my drive.

Now I freely use fly spray, on mossies as well,
and I wish all the bush rats a slow roast in hell.
Oh and as for that Buddha, now God's on my side
I'll take my revenge down at Kentucky Fried.

from **Spacewalk**

The Vast Importance of Knowing a Little

The first story tells of a dreamtime tree, felled.
Its honey-dripping branches spread out and down an escarpment,
and so seawards the first creeks and rivers formed.
It's a pre-history of metaphor, and then science:
the recognition of properties shared by disparate things
the gradual force of principles fixed in memory.
Second is Dad's idea of a joke: the engineer who charged
five thousand and five for a chalk mark – five, he said,
for the mark and the chalk; five thousand for knowing where it goes.
Ho ho, and in the third, salmon gums line salt lakes and graded roads.
Muscle-pink even when the sky is steely, their shadows
splay like veins across the gravel. And this lake is
blinding white, and it leaks a mirage onto the road,
and there is a fallen tree, and the brain doesn't know
what the eye cannot see, and the young woman, driving too fast,
swerves rolls and lies fixed by the wheat belt's silence, and her car.
Fourthly, in wavering time we have her bloodless on the bed,
vaguely conscious, no pulse, no blood pressure.
Hours have collapsed. Still she rolls away from us;
neural streams in her salt-water body stagnating,
sinews of consequence tightening, but there in my mind
lies propped my formalin-stained Cunningham's *Manual
of Practical Anatomy*, open beside an opened hand
as my hands were learning how to trust themselves,
to follow their fingers, to trace upstream
and back to life the slender cloistered vessels,
the arching trees of arterioles and veins, the delicate
basket that steels the hand, the very weft of blood
that powers the fist that grips the wheel. And my hands
learned what should be firm and what should yield;

where there is symmetry and where there is not. And later
I learned that after that anxious sweat, the saline drip
blindly placed, to look again, O comely lass from Ireland,
dying right before me. So where was your right hip? And
why the bone in your belly? And where did you hide your blood?
It's all right. I know your rivers and where their tributaries run.
Painstakingly, and years ago, I assembled a picture of you
from the inside. My teachers in anatomy were both alive,
and dead. The plane from Perth dropped in, and you survived.
And after that a violent wind winnowed the wheat belt
and an enormous willy-willy lifted Lake Grace (pure
white salt and as dead as you like) and flounced and folded
and downed it like a brand-new hospital blanket.
And in my car distinction blurred then drowned. The sky lost
the wheat and the trees, and I felt honoured to have been threshed
by the storm, crystalline and abrasive.
And strangely then I remembered our professor, Darian-Smith,
his studies of touch and manual dexterity,
and his monkeys that travelled with him, eyes fixed on the road ahead,
fingers tracing the future's mirage.

Spacewalk

From way out here, and off to one side,
the Earth is an eyeball, cyclones eyelids
batting. It rolls along its squinty elliptic,
an orbital edge bone-solid as Newton's physics.
Solar wind broils and warps about
its shimmering magnetosphere.

The Sun and Earth together stare
out at some stars our imagination
has already flown beyond. Earth's dark side
flickers like neurons firing deep
in the retina. Light-side's a blazing
skyscape, sunbeams and the weft
of our own light too bright to watch.
Too often we look at our feet.

Astronauts, our hopes and fears projected,
float for us, camera-hatted, like reflective
bodies in space; like third eyes taking in everything
then sifting through the hay bale galaxies
for a needle pointing north to something
that doesn't bounce our faces back.
Something finally outside ourselves.

The Racing Heart

Round and round the great grey
hooping highways of Australia
a horse is driven in a white box
to be backed into a brown stall
only to trot a grass-green circle
as red-faced people bob up and down
under a truly blue sky
flagging their diminished currency
and holding on to hat brims
any colour at all.

Weeding Coolumbooka

'Dusk deepens, sturdy pines stand firm.' Mao Tse Tung, 1961

Dense and regimented stand the pines;
quiet underneath, frost lingers.
Darkly they take root in Coolumbooka,
their needles softly suffocate Westringias.
With those masters of the T'ang, I admire
the pine trees' evergreen resilience,
but if I let them grow much higher
they'll be too tough, they'll uproot the fence.

We pull them up and cut them back, these pines;
by axe and saw, by hand we push them back;
we prop the fences and clean the signs
and curse the feral dogs and deer and pigs and cats.
And so it is we kill to keep the bush alive:
then home to dream in our Japanese four-wheel drive.

Resurface

Snow gums drawl like roll-your-owns,
they sag from lips: granite boulders
countless mouths of the buried.

A lean feral dog offends the bush.
Trucks rumble subsoil with their horizontal logs.
Road crew smoko and expletives crack like ice.

Their great stiff-bristle brooms stammer
at the gravel, and boiling beads of bitumen
skitter across the junction's surface.

Cold and wet, sun and moon stare down
the sky's rifle barrel, and the smoke
hangs where it was exhaled.

So cold a stubbie ex-esky is capable
of warming hands, while the smoke, like the town
forty ks south, gradually dissipates.

This is no place for pausing to consider.
The day is overtaking us, and back in town
the kids are being driven to their destinies.

A wombat ambles across the line-marker's dream.
The road dozes right on through us.
The trucks never stop bringing in supplies.

Last Stop Bombala

Back then, & had I confused the signs?
But at last I heard the old steam train,
& the aching rails quiver…
& now I walk between the lines,
& still I watch my back and shiver

& though today the sky can't find the rain
I feel content (having left the mind
waiting on its platform, for history to deliver),
and the frost, if not the sun, shines
through the shunting yard by the river

& ease needs no epiphany
& the fog cannot withstand the sun,
and this journey is ever new to me
like those disembarking kids and their fresh-faced fun.

Uncollected

Black Stump

for Aunty Joy Robinson

Fire in the willows, &
the white man sprints to pumps;
the foxes and the rabbits split
& the conflagration jumps –
over sheep that sleep like pillows,
across the farms it shows no pity –
the orange sky is over-lit –
now hungry flames lick to the city.
I walked across the river bed
where the platypus are penned;
where white man wrecked the watershed
moaning 'when will this drought end?'
At last it's White Australia's turn:
let's hope we blacken as we burn.

Mother sonnet

My mother didn't want me.
Sometimes she told me so.
She was only being honest
I know.

I always did my best
to work away the pain;
I fronted up to life
again and again.

It's taken years to understand,
years to steady my hand;
it's taken time to forgive
and to complete my growth.

This could have been while she still lived:
this poem is to release us both.

A Farewell to Country

Snow-melt runnels the char-trunk forest,
ferals run the breathing land down.
Nervous epicormic buds. No little fish to eye me
trampling someone else's unkempt garden.

I acknowledge, also, the cattle-ravaged hinterland,
& that contemplation fades in this dog-soiled soundscape,
& that city light washes the stars out, back
into the dust from which they were extruded, & that
language shuffles on the wordy deck.

Farewell! Fare well? How can I say it?
To a country I never really met? & how
could it hear me, when it's already on its way?
& how to stop the rain that's running now
down the other side of Nature's face?

www.ingramcontent.com/pod-product-compliance
Lightning Source LLC
Chambersburg PA
CBHW071438080526
44587CB00014B/1894